AN INVITATION
TO
RELIGIOUS EDUCATION

AN INVITATION TO RELIGIOUS EDUCATION

HAROLD WILLIAM BURGESS

RELIGIOUS EDUCATION PRESS
BIRMINGHAM, ALABAMA 35209

Printed in the United States of America

Library of Congress Catalog Card Number: 75-14980

ISBN: 0-89135-019-5

10 9 8 7 6

Religious Education Press, Inc.
1531 Wellington Road
Birmingham, Alabama 35209

Religious Education Press Inc. publishes books and educational materials exclusively in religious education and in areas closely related to religious education. It is committed to enhancing and professionalizing religious education through the publication of significant scholarly and popular books.

CONTENTS

To William K. Burgess
my father

FOREWORD

The study of religious education, long a tradition in Protestant seminaries, has more recently become an area of concentration for Catholic colleges and state institutions of higher education. In Protestant seminaries, where the task has been to prepare individuals to conduct the educational enterprise of the parish, religious education has attempted to gain a *professional* orientation. Over the past several years, with the reduction of its parochial school system, the Catholic Church has turned to its colleges and universities for guidance in establishing a distinctly religious educational endeavor. In this collegiate setting, religious education has had the potential for gaining an *academic* orientation. State universities, responding to the insistent public call for religious or ethical education and spurred on by the Supreme Court's decision to allow teaching about religion in public schools, have likewise directed considerable attention towards religious education. These universities have been able to focus on the *objective* distinction between the broader notion of religious education (which prepares one to encounter the phenomenon of the religious aspect of man's nature) and the more confessional conception of religious education (which aims to prepare one for religious life in a particular sect). These three approaches to the study of religious education portend great promise for the future of religious education as a profession, as a discipline, and as a field.

In each of the above situations, however, religious education is fighting for its life. With the decline of the Sunday School in "mainline" Protestant denominations, and with a consequent lack of denominational support, a number of Protestant seminary departments of religious education are being phased out.

In Catholic colleges and universities, the situation can be compared to that of the biblical proverb of the sower and the seed where the seed was planted on rocky soil and sprang up fast only to die away just as quickly. Catholic collegiate programs for the study of religious education, in like manner, were hastily put together; but, without the roots of scholarly tradition typical of other collegiate programs, few are finding themselves able to survive the present period of economic consolidation. In state institutions, religious education constitutes an innovation which arises at the very time when severe declines in funding and enrollment tend to place innovative programs lowest on the list of priorities.

The lack of scholarly foundation is the basic reason for the precarious state of religious education in seminaries, colleges, and universities. In Protestant seminaries, for example, religious education gained scholarly standing principally through its association with theology. This is not to deny that solid scholarship has been done by religious educators in this tradition. From Horace Bushnell to Robert Lynn there is a sufficient number of names to make a most impressive litany. But, being professionally oriented, religious education never earned the academic standing of such traditional subjects as philosophy and theology.

Unfortunately, in Catholic college and university settings, the religious education field has been far from universally successful. Although most of these institutions have come to accept the position that religious education has its own *raison d'etre* distinct from theology, financial considerations have tended to make Catholic religious educators more concerned with selling religious education programs than with scholarship. Consequently, the field has been made subject to the market—a market unable to provide support for the caliber of research required to establish religious education as a scholarly discipline.

In public institutions, religious education has not yet found its home. There, it is sometimes split between a department of religious studies and a school of education. Such an arrangement is likely to lack departmental interaction. Individuals in religious studies tend to be "scientific-objective" researchers while those in education tend to be interested in pedagogical

matters, the technicalities of state certification, etc. Few programs in state institutions, then, have concerned themselves
with synthetic research. And, it is only by such deliberate integration of theory and practice that the scholarly justification for
a field of study can be established.

Harold William Burgess' *An Invitation to Religious Education* is
addressed directly to this problem of establishing a scholarly
foundation for the field of religious education. Going further
than simply notifying us of the problem, this book takes *the*
fundamental step towards solving the problem: *it raises the
theory-practice relationship to the level of consciousness.* By providing
religious educators a framework within which to articulate their
intentions and consequent practice, Burgess invites us to begin
speaking with a unified language. His work presents the possibility of ending religious education's Babel period of confused
tongues by making it clear that, in religious education, the
connection between theory and practice is not an "either/or,"
but a "both/and." That is, what we intend (whether consciously
or not) shows up in our practice.

Through his examination of the theoretical literature in religious education, Burgess identifies four distinct approaches to
religious education: the traditional theological approach, the
social-cultural approach, the contemporary theological approach, and the social-science approach. He then develops a
system of investigative categories to identify and relate specific
characteristics of these various theoretical approaches. With the
employment of these categories, Burgess seeks to pinpoint the
theoretical and practical position of each approach relative to
aim, content, teacher, student, environment, and evaluation. As
we read his work, then, we begin to see similar patterns of
thought in the writings of such theorists as Gaebelein, LeBar,
Mason, Jungmann, Hofinger, and van Caster; in Coe, Bower,
and Chave; and in Miller, Sherrill, Smart, and Moran. Burgess'
efforts can be summarized in a 4 x 6 matrix (in which the four
rows comprise the theoretical approaches and the six columns
comprise the categories of religious education practice).

Although he treats the social-science type in every bit as
objective a fashion as the others, Burgess does share with us his
bias for this theoretical approach. He does this both by demon-

strating how this approach might well afford the best opportunity for establishing a definable field and by employing the social-science mode of procedure in the study itself. Burgess has thereby not only provided us with a study of the four selected approaches to religious education, but also with a process by which we can understand yet other theoretical approaches in their relation to educational practice.

An Invitation marks a new level of scholarship in religious education in that it brings us to that stage in the development of a science (the paradigmatic stage) at which we can begin to self-reflect in a systematic way on our theory and practice. As with all true scholarship, this work will have its effect not only upon those engaged in higher education, but it will also aid the religion teacher because it goes right to the heart of the act of teaching—the point of contact between teacher and student. Here, it will aid the teacher to become conscious of the relationship between what he intends and what he does.

Robert T. O'Gorman
St. Thomas Seminary
Denver, Colorado

Chapter I

The Problem

A CRITICAL NEED IN RELIGIOUS EDUCATION

Not everybody knows what religious education is.[1] Despite numerous attempts to define the field, an apparent identity problem exists for religious education.[2] One critic of the religious education scene remarks that even the scholarly authorities in the field, namely those who write the journal articles and author the statements in denominational handbooks, are not able to give a satisfactory answer to the question "what is religious education?"[3]

An examination of current statements of religious educational purpose indicates that, in addition to being unable to define religious education satisfactorily, religious educationists[4] are also hardpressed to say clearly what it is supposed to do.[5] One factor contributing to this perplexity concerning the understanding of the nature and purposes of religious education seems to be that religious educationists have a difficult time communicating with each other because common principles of formulation and methodology of study have been neglected.[6]

In contrast with this state of affairs where not even the authorities can say for sure what religious education is, one philosopher of science can boldly assert that everybody knows what science is because everybody knows what science does.[7] Science observes, discovers, measures, experiments, and frames theories about the way and why of things. A typical scientist in any of the scientific disciplines is trained in a rigorous system whereby he has become confident and skillful. In particular, he has acquired a knowledge of theory and a method of applying theory in practice. Hence, the scientist knows how to formulate

1

his goals and how to progress toward them. He is also able to communicate clearly with other scientists.

An important reason for the problem of definition and identity within the field of religious education is that the conscious attention to theory together with its application in practice which has enabled the scientist to clearly formulate his goals and to progress toward them has not been achieved by religious educationists on a scale which is broad enough to bridge denominational and theological lines in such a way as to establish valid boundaries for the field of religious education.[8] Thus, religious educationists need not be surprised that some persons do not know what religious education is, and that the field is lightly regarded by others.

The current literature of the profession, however, exhibits a hopeful awareness of the need to attend to matters of theory. There is also evidence of a developing commitment on the part of religious educationists to engage in reflection upon the implications of such matters. D. Campbell Wyckoff, long concerned with the theoretical problems of religious education from a Protestant perspective, clearly expresses the present attitude of a significant number of religious educationists: "The most critical problem that faces Christian education, however, is its need to understand itself—to gain deep insight into what it is about. It needs to see how it is related to the cultural situation, to the church's life and thought, and to the educational process. This problem of self-understanding is the problem of theory."[9]

The Roman Catholic religious educationist, James Michael Lee, suggests that there is nothing more important for the field of religious education than the development of a good and useful theory.[10] In Europe a somewhat similar concern is expressed, albeit from a different perspective, by Hubert Halbfas, also a Roman Catholic.[11]

In a monograph setting forth the educational philosophy of the theologically conservative National Union of Christian Schools, Nicholas Henry Beversluis proposes that engaging in theoretical activity could ultimately prove to be one of the more relevant and practical concerns for Christian education.[12] Lawrence Little, for many years engaged in the education of

persons preparing for professional positions in religious education, likewise speaks strongly of the need for dealing specifically
with theoretical issues as they relate to religious education.[13]

Additional impetus for the development of religious educational theory has come from articles and symposia that are
published regularly in *Religious Education,* the official journal of
the Religious Education Association.[14] These articles and symposia typically reflect the concern of notable scholars with
respect to the casual attitude toward theory which often un-
derlies practice in the work of religious education. Another
project of the Religious Education Association, namely, *Research
on Religious Development: A Comprehensive Handbook,* dramatically
emphasizes the need to achieve a higher level of theoretical
sophistication in the field of religious education as a basis for
pursuing meaningful research. Merton Strommen, editor of
the *Handbook,* reports that only a few of the thousands of studies
initially reviewed for this project were guided by clearly stated
theories or responsible hypotheses.[15]

The present work seeks to respond to the widely recognized
critical need to deal with the matter of theory in the field of
religious education. It does not, however, attempt to formulate
a particular theory. Rather it is an effort to make more explicit
the theoretical elements which tend to be characteristic of
certain theoretical approaches to religious education which are
discernable in the professional literature.

One factor which influences this investigation is that the
notion of "theory" is itself a somewhat slippery concept. Philosophical and scientific uses of the word, for example, differ.[16]
Not only does the word have a wide range of connotations, but,
as Elizabeth Steiner Maccia demonstrates, theory may include
such diverse focuses as speculation with respect to structure,
occurrence, value, or practice.[17]

The term "theory" is derived from the Greek word Θεωρὶα
signifying "a beholding" or "a speculation." A normal contemporary usage of the word "theory" refers to a verified explanation of a set of facts as they relate to one another. By extension of
this usage, theory provides a plausible explanation of the principles underlying a particular practice.[18] A typical definition of
theory, as used in the behavioral sciences, is that proposed by

Fred Kerlinger: "A theory is a set of interrelated constructs (concepts), definitions, and propositions that presents a systematic view of phenomena by specifying relations among variables, with the purpose of explaining and predicting the phenomena."[19]

Even if religious educationists could agree on a basic definition of theory, such as that of Kerlinger, they probably would have a considerable difference of opinion with respect to the specific constructs, definitions, and propositions which are necessary for the development of a theory suitable to their individual understanding of the nature and aims of religious education. Some religious educationists, for example, are essentially concerned with the handing on of a divine message.[20] Other theorists focus their attention upon immediate social issues.[21] Still other theorists propose that a theologically valid and educationally sound theory must be developed from the interaction of theology and the science of education.[22] Another suggests that it is the teaching-learning process which is the core of a fruitful theory of religious education.[23] From this cursory summary of approaches to theorizing about religious education, it is not hard to see that attempts to communicate amid these differing views may well be cacophonous.

In an endeavor to promote more meaningful theoretical activity and more effective communication within the field of religious education, one purpose of this work is to investigate ways in which major schools of thought agree or disagree with respect to the constructs, definitions, and propositions which constitute common elements in religious educational theory. In order to achieve this objective, a system of investigative categories will be employed as an analytical tool for the purpose of identifying and relating salient characteristics of the several theoretical approaches.

Obviously the task of ordering and disciplining the wealth of theory and practical knowledge already in existence will not be exhausted in the present study, but a preliminary explanation of various theoretical approaches is well worth the effort as one means of better understanding the present state of theorizing among religious educationists. A related benefit of this work is that it develops a common set of constructs which might well become the basis for a more adequate level of communication among religious educationists.

THEORY AND PRACTICE IN RELIGIOUS EDUCATION

Relationship of theory and practice

The establishment of an appropriate relationship between theory and practice is a perennial problem in religious education, as it is in other disciplines. The ancient Greeks first advanced the notion of a possible relationship between theory and practice. For the Greeks, theory and practice referred to modes of life which, though polar opposites, were not separate. "Theoretical" life included what would today be called "scientific inquiry." This "scientific inquiry" was not rooted in mere curiosity, nor in practical necessity. It was rather to escape ignorance. "Practical" life, for the Greeks, was concerned with the performing of activities. Twentieth century language practices have resulted in a quite different popular understanding of the relation of practice to theory. As Nicholas Lobkowicz observes: "When today we oppose 'practice' to 'theory' we usually have in mind lived life as opposed to abstract ideas, or else man's acting as opposed to his 'mere' thinking and reflecting."[24] The common usage, described by Lobkowicz, has the effect of causing what is thought to be a practical notion to appear more valuable, or more useful, than a theoretical notion.

Possibly influenced by a popular rather than a scientific attitude toward theory, religious educationists typically have divorced practice from theory. Indeed, it is not uncommon in certain circles for practice to be elevated above theory. In any case, the separation of theory and practice constitutes one of the principal reasons why religious education has had a difficult time establishing itself as a profession.[25] A striking example of that mentality which has contributed to the divorcement of theory and practice within the field of religious education is found in the "Introductory" to the first issue of *Religious Education* (April, 1906): "Religious Education has no academic problem. There are plenty of philosophers who will take care of the theoretical aspects of the subject. The Religious Education

Association stands for practice rather than theory, experience rather than speculation."[26] There seems to be substantial evidence to suggest that religious educationists typically have followed this kind of mentality. By adopting a stance which minimizes the importance of the relationship between theory and practice, they have opted for practical rather than for theoretical concerns.

This "bias toward the practical" has been pinpointed by Charles Melchert as a fundamental crisis within the field of religious education attributable to the lack of theoretical and conceptual clarity on the part of religious educationists.[27] In the field of religious education, according to Melchert, a decision to change a practice merely means that "one decides to do it differently."[28] This change process, by leaving little room for the consideration of theoretical or empirical grounds which might justify either the change or the new practice, contributes only sparingly to the fund of knowledge by which religious educational practices could be guided. The problem with a practice not solidly based on theory is that it has no sources which would encourage educational enrichment, change, and reconstruction on a basis more solid than whim and fancy. Furthermore, too close a tie to practice typically results in a myopic perspective with reference to objectives. Consequently, evaluation of results is difficult. "Consistent Christian education practice must thus," in the words of D. Campbell Wyckoff, "be based upon an informed and responsible theory."[29]

The all-too-common failure to base religious education practices on informed and responsible theory has an additional consequence, namely this: when theoretical foundations for religious education practices are not articulated explicitly, the reasons for the selection of one practice and not another are likely to remain unclear to the educationist who must make the selection. Unless the theoretical rationale is understood, the learning outcomes of a specific practice may be quite different from the ones intended by the educationist who proposed the practice. The religious educationist, James Michael Lee, sees this failure to connect theory and practice as a major factor contributing to the relative inefficiency of much religious education.[30] In fact, Lee suggests, it is quite possible for religion teachers holding one theory of religious instruction to draw pedagogical practices from another highly conflicting theory, in effect, compounding the problem.[31] In this connection, as Robert Boehlke reminds us, even the most "practical" person operates on the basis of some theory whether he is fully aware of it or not.[32]

From what has been already adduced, it may be safely concluded that religious education, as a professional activity, will be raised to a higher level by recognizing and articulating the dependency of theory and practice upon each other. Theory which remains in the realm of speculation and practice which is unaware of the theory upon which it is based are equally unproductive of renewing and developing the field of religious education. On the other hand, a creative and responsible use of theory coupled with a conscious awareness of the theoretical implications of practices that are employed will enhance the professional status of the field. In addition, religious educational theory and practice can more fruitfully contribute to each other.[33]

The establishment of a system of categories that will promote the meshing of theory and practice in the field of religious education is among the interests of this work. Such a system should enable theoreticians and practitioners to communicate more clearly. An additional benefit might well be the adoption of a less esoteric and more precise language than is sometimes employed among religious educationists. The use of more understandable language would, in turn, enable religious educationists to speak more effectively to the workaday religion teacher as well as to the public at large.

Available scientific tools not used by religious educationists

Religious educationists tend to be characterized not only by the previously mentioned "bias toward the practical" but also by their typical use of impressionistic evidence as a basis for selecting and evaluating religious education practices.[34] Reliance upon this kind of "soft" evidence is not likely to provide a foundation for such an interaction of theory and practice as might result in the desired renewal of religious education and consequently in the advancement of the field as a profession. However, techniques developed in the social sciences afford the possibility of replacing the rather subjective information typically relied upon by religious educationists engaged in change processes with objective, empirically derived, "hard" evidence which could provide a base for a more meaningful interaction of theory and practice than has been characteristic of the theoretical process within the field of religious education.[35]

The applicability of social science methodology to the investigation of issues relevant to religious educational concerns has been demonstrated by studies such as the Character Education Inquiry, a project directed during the 1920's by Hugh Hartshorne and Mark A. May.[36] These studies, in addition to showing that empirical methods could be used to evaluate the results of religious education practices, also demonstrated that theoretical notions upon which religious education practices have been based are likewise open to examination. For example, the Hartshorne and May studies brought serious question to the validity of one theoretical assumption evident in the literature of religious education at least as far back as Augustine's *De Catechizandis Rudibus*,[37] a treatise written early in the fifth century. This assumption, upon which religious educationists have typically placed a great deal of confidence, is that a person is almost always able to transfer knowledge of morals and religious ideals into his own personal way of living. The Hartshorne and May investigation, in fact, revealed little correlation between knowledge of religious ideals and actual moral behavior.[38]

By the middle of the twentieth century, the demonstrated feasibility of applying scientific methods to theoretical concerns of religious education had delivered religious educationists from the necessity of relying upon mere impressions and subjective judgments when changes seemed to be indicated. Hence, the way was open for reliable empirical testing of theoretical notions before putting them in practice on a large scale. The establishment of a framework for theorizing and for testing hypotheses in a scientific manner was a logical "next step." Such a framework would have enabled religious educationists to develop their capacity to make use of theory to bring about more fruitful practices; and, incidentally, it would have provided a genuine professional service to the church.

However, the above-mentioned step of establishing a viable, ongoing means of making use of available scientific methodology to advance the cause of religious education has not, even as yet, been taken. Pertinent to this point is Andrè Godin's comment to the effect that among religious educationists everything goes along just as though experimental techniques did not exist.[39] Godin, having surveyed a decade of research literature, concludes that: "Not a single study has been published as a dissertation at either the master's or the doctor's level which has taken for its object the evaluation of the pedagogical effectiveness of a method of religious education . . . and has demonstrated the superiority of this method over another."[40] The situation, as analyzed by Godin, appears little improved.[41]

One reason for the slow development of a framework for both theorizing and hypothesis testing in the field of religious education is that the necessary descriptive research underlying this phase of theorizing has not been fully accomplished. Carter Good and Douglas Scates speak to this point in suggesting that research progress in a given field may wait more on sound theory, developed from the process of "descriptive analysis," than it does upon instrumentation.[42] In a similar vein, Robert Dubin expresses his opinion that descriptive research yields the "stuff" which the theorist uses in the development of the units which make up his theories.[43]

This work, then, in addition to previously stated aims, proposes to engage in a descriptive analytical study of the theorizing of representative religious educationists concerning some fundamental units of religious education, for example: aim, content, and environment. Such a descriptive analysis should contribute to the fruitful use of scientific methodologies already available to religious educationists.

A PROPOSAL FOR ANALYZING THEORETICAL APPROACHES TO RELIGIOUS EDUCATION

A category system

Since religious education writings are often characterized by lack of clarity, it would appear helpful to employ a system of investigative categories in order to facilitate the analysis and description of approaches to theorizing about religious education as proposed in this work. The development of such a framework of categories has been suggested as possibly the most immediately fruitful step for those within the field of religious education.[44]

The notion of a category system as a device for explaining religious educational theory is not a new one in the field. George Coe, for example, uses a kind of category system as a means of presenting his theoretical proposals in his widely read book, *A Social Theory of Religious Education.*[45] The components of religious education theory used by Coe in *A Social Theory* are: *first,* an indication of the kind of society that is regarded as a desirable end result of religious education; *second,* a notion of the original nature of the student; *third,* an idea of the kinds of educational experiences that will most surely bring about the desired result; and *fourth,* some means by which progress is evaluated.[46] There is good reason to believe that the continuing influence of George Coe as a religious educational theorist rests, in part, on the cogent presentation of his views made possible by the careful ordering of his theory according to its elements.

D. Campbell Wyckoff proposes a category framework consisting of six basic units as a means of understanding and expressing religious education theory. His units are: (1) objective, (2) scope, (3) context, (4) process, (5) personnel, and (6) timing.[47] Wyckoff contends that the use and further development of this, or some other similar categorization, is a necessary step in the development of religious education as discipline.[48] It is interesting to note Wyckoff's belief that the questions reflected in his proposed category framework are ultimately theological questions and that they may be answered as biblical studies, history, theology, and ethics are taken into account.[49] Xavier Harris uses the following units in his analysis of the theory of religious instruction in Catholic secondary schools: (1) aim, (2) teacher, (3) student, (4) curriculum, and (5) methods.[50] J. Gordon Chamberlin, an observer and analyst of the religious education scene, examines the context in which church education is carried out with a type of category approach composed of the following considerations: *first,* an examination of the context in which church education is carried on; *second,* an examination of the relation between the fields of education and theology; *third,* an examination of the ends or objectives of the educational enterprise; and *fourth,* an examination of the processes of education.[51]

Three "first order questions" in the consideration of religious educational theory are proposed by Nicholas Henry Beversluis: *first,* what should be the school's religious vision? *second,* what should be its major learning goals? and *third,* what should be its core of required subjects?[52] Lewis Joseph Sherrill distinguishes among four perennial efforts of religious men to provide a basis for a comparative study of religious beliefs and education: ". . . the attempt to discern the nature of the Supreme Being, the attempt to discover how he manifests himself most significantly, the attempt to know what his will for men is, and the attempt to identify and secure the ultimate values of the universe."[53]

James Michael Lee analyzes the teaching of religion in terms of four categories: *first,* the environment; *second,* the student; *third,* the teacher; and *fourth,* the subject matter.[54] Charles Hardie concludes that four conceptions are basic to any educational theory: *first,* the original nature of man; *second,* the production of changes in behavior, for example, the formation of habits; *third,* the environment, and *fourth,* the idea of value.[55]

The several styles of categorization suggested by these writers for the study of and expression of religious education in its theoretical dimensions tend to reflect the thought patterns and expository notions of the writers who propose them. For this reason, and in the absence of a universally agreed-upon set of units or categories, the present work will employ the following set of categories as an analytical device to facilitate the proposed analysis and description of selected theoretical approaches to religious education: (1) aim, (2) content, (3) teacher, (4) student, (5) environment, and (6) evaluation. No claim is made that this category system is exhaustive of the possibilities. The six categories here employed do embody several notions evident in the category frameworks previously reviewed. However, the responsibility for the selection of these particular units rests with the present writer.

Some clarifications

". . . Back of almost everything that gets figured out in head-quarters are some ideas that were first developed in the minds and experiences of those who produced thoughtful books."[56] In accord with this observation by Kendig Brubaker Cully, a perceptive analyst of the religious education scene, this work is based on an analysis of the religious educational thought found in books written by selected religious educationists who have been influential in shaping the thought processes in the field of religious education during the twentieth century. The decision to focus the attention of the present work upon the twentieth century is based upon evidence that the early years of the century witnessed a period of change which resulted, eventually, in the crystalizing of identifiable approaches to theorizing about religious education. The works of religious education theorists from a broad spectrum of Christian traditions, both Protestant and Roman Catholic, are included in this investigation. One reason for including the theoretical works of several traditions is that religious educationists, if they are to provide a professional service to many church traditions, must understand the thinking of these traditions in order to communicate with them. In this connection, it is to be regretted that the present study is limited to an examination of theoretical works written from an essentially Christian perspective.

Though this work intends to participate in a theoretical activity, the use of the word "theory" as a fundamental part of the vocabulary gives rise to certain difficulties. William Bedford Williamson, for example, demonstrates numerous language problems attendant upon discussions of "theory" in the field of religious education.[57] Furthermore, few religious educationists seem to make explicit enunciation of their theory as theory. In recognition of these, and related problems arising from the use of the word "theory" in connection with the present investigation, the construct "theoretical approach" rather than the word "theory" will be employed to specify what might also be called a "school of thought." More specifically, "theoretical approach" will include the following categories of thought common to theorizing about religious education: aim, content, teacher, student, environment, and evaluation.

The proposed analysis of the selected theoretical approaches, then, will follow the pattern of examining books of religious educationists identified with the several approaches in order to ascertain the typical theoretical position of the several approaches with respect to: *first,* the aim of religious education, which in this preliminary investigation will also include such notions as goal, purpose, objective, and the like; *second,* the content of religious education (the nature of content is perceived so differently among religious educationists, that, of necessity, the scope of this category will not be the same for each approach—for example, one school of thought identifies content with a divine message while another school of thought identifies content directly with the religious instruction act);[58] *third,* the role of the teacher in the teaching of religion; *fourth,* the student, particularly the manner in which he acquires and in which he manifests religious learning outcomes; *fifth,* the function of the environment in religious education; and *sixth,* the means by which religious education may be evaluated.

Four theoretical approaches

The four approaches to theorizing about religious education which will be described and analyzed in this work are: "the traditional theological approach," "the social-cultural approach," "the contemporary theological approach," and "the social-science approach." Although these approaches are not exhaustive of the possibilities for discriminating among ways of designating schools of thought concerning religious education, they do seem to be etched out in religious educational literature with sufficient clarity to warrant this preliminary descriptive-analytical investigation.

Three schools of religious educational thought delineated by Harrison Elliott in *Can Religious Education Be Christian?*[59] are typical of classifications made by several other religious educationists, both Protestant and Catholic.[60] The first school of thought described by Elliott is founded upon the traditions and longstanding practices of the church, as well as upon normative theological considerations. Theoretical concerns of this approach, according to Elliott, center upon how the message of the church may be more effectively presented. Elliott associates

the second school of thought with the so-called religious education movement and its characteristic use of educational insights
rather than theological conceptualizations in the development
of religious educational practices. Instead of focusing its attention upon religious education as a methodology for the transmission of a message, this approach centers its interest upon
social and cultural development. The third school of thought in
Elliott's scheme emphasizes what he terms a "neo-orthodox"
theological interpretation of both the Christian religion and of
Christian education.[61]

In addition to the three schools of thought delineated by
Harrison Elliott, and by other educationists in similar fashion, a
fourth approach based on the social sciences may be observed in
religious educational literature. The first presentation of a
distinctly social-science approach to religious education theory
to appear in book form was made in several chapters of *Toward a
Future for Religious Education*,[62] edited by James Michael Lee and
Patrick Rooney. In the Foreword of *Toward a Future*, Lee writes:
"This book represents an approach to catechetics which some of
us believe is at once unique and new. The approach I am
referring to is the social-science approach to religious instruction."[63] The social-science approach, which is radicated in the
teaching-learning process, accepts the content of theology and
inserts it, as pedogogically appropriate, into the approach.

The four approaches to theorizing about religious education
which are selected for the present descriptive analysis follow
closely the three schools of thought identified by Harrison
Elliott in *Can Religious Education Be Christian?* with the addition
of the fourth school of thought proposed by James Michael Lee
in the Foreword of *Toward a Future for Religious Education*. It may
be noted that although there is an historical progression in the
development of the four approaches it would be misleading to
say that these approaches are equivalent to historical periods.

SUMMARY OF THEORETICAL APPROACHES

The following chapters will set forth the background and
characteristics of the four selected theoretical approaches to
religious education more completely. Nevertheless, a brief summary at this point may be helpful.

The traditional theological theoretical approach to religious education may be said to be primarily concerned with the communication of a divine message. Theology is normative for all decisions relative to matters of theory and practice. This approach typically gives rise to forms of practice linked to a lecture or preaching model.

The social-cultural theoretical approach to religious education is based upon the progressive educational theories and liberal theology characteristic of the so-called religious education movement as evident in the writings of such authors as George Coe, William Clayton Bower, and Ernest Chave. This approach is sometimes referred to in Protestant literature as an educational approach because educational insights rather than theological conceptualizations are usually used by social-cultural theorists in the theoretical process. Practices generated within this theoretical approach are typically oriented to life through social activity.

The contemporary theological theoretical approach to religious education focuses upon an organic relationship between religious education and the Christian community. Theology, though conceptualized in several ways by representative theorists, is considered normative for all matters of theory and practice. Some influential religious educationists who have been instrumental in the shaping of this approach are Randolph Crump Miller, Lewis Sherrill, James Smart, and Gabriel Moran. The wide variety of theological and educational thought among contemporary theological theorists contributes to an eclectic pattern of religious educational practice. However, practices developed directly out of the mainstream of this theoretical approach typically feature relational group activities in which the group (class) is considered a microcosm of the church.

The social-science theoretical approach to religious education is rooted in the teaching-learning process. As a religious educational theory it sustains a value-free relationship to theology, the content of theology being accepted and inserted, as appropriate, into the approach. Practices generated from within the social-science approach have a high degree of specificity to individual situations; they flow from the deliberative effort of the religion teacher to use environmental factors in the here-

and-now learning process to effect selected, behaviorally defined, student learning outcomes. James Michael Lee is the only religious educationist to have written books from a specifically social-science frame of reference.

Notes for Chapter I

1. The decision to employ the term "religious education" rather than "Christian education" or "catechetics" represents an effort to use as broad a term as possible. No particular nuance is intended. For a relevant discussion of terminology, see James Michael Lee, *The Shape of Religious Instruction* (Dayton, Ohio: Pflaum, 1971), pp. 6-8.

2. One example is George Albert Coe, *What Is Christian Education?* (New York: Scribner's, 1929).

3. William Bedford Williamson, *Language and Concepts in Christian Education* (Philadelphia: Westminster, 1970), pp. 33-37.

4. The term "religious educationist" refers to a person who is expert in religious educational theory and practice, especially one who has written books or scholarly articles on theoretical matters in the field of religious education.

5. William Bedford Williamson has reported on such an examination in which the principles of linguistic and concept analysis were applied to typical statements of aim/goals/objectives/purposes drawn from both institutional and individual sources, *Language and Concepts in Christian Education*, especially pp. 37-41.

6. J. Gordon Chamberlin, *Freedom and Faith* (Philadelphia: Westminster, 1965), p. 20.

7. Marx W. Wartofsky, *Conceptual Foundations of Scientific Thought: An Introduction to the Philosophy of Science* (New York: Macmillan, 1968), p. 1.

8. For an extended discussion of this issue, see the symposia "Religious Education as a Discipline," *Religious Education*, LXII (September-October, 1967) pp. 387-430, and "Crisis and Hope in Religious Education," *Religious Education*, LXVII (September-October, 1972), especially pp. 359-374.

9. D. Campbell Wyckoff, *The Gospel and Christian Education* (Philadelphia: Westminster, 1959), p. 7.

10. James Michael Lee, *The Flow of Religious Instruction* (Dayton, Ohio: Pflaum/Standard, 1973), p. 272.

11. Hubert Halbfas, *Theory of Catechetics* (New York: Herder and Herder, 1971).

12. Nicholas Henry Beversluis, *Christian Philosophy of Education* (Grand Rapids, Michigan: National Union of Christian Schools, 1971), p. 17.

13. Lawrence C. Little, *Foundations for a Philosophy of Christian Education* (New York: Abingdon, 1962), especially p. 17.

14. Particularly relevant are the symposia "Religious Education as a Discipline," *Religious Education*, LXII (September-October, 1967), pp. 387-430; and "Crisis and Hope in Religious Education," *Religious Education*, LXVII (September-October, 1972), pp. 323-395. Also see C. Ellis Nelson, "Is Church Education Something Particular," *Religious Education*, LXVII (January-February, 1972), pp. 5-16.

15. Merton P. Strommen, editor, *Research on Religious Development* (New York: Hawthorne, 1971), p. xviii.

16. Compare the scholastic definition of theory in Bernard Wuellnar, *Dictionary of Scholastic Philosophy* (Milwaukee: Bruce, 1956), p. 124, with the use of theory in Stephen Toulmin, *The Philosophy of Science* (London: Hutchinson, 1953), pp. 105-139.

17. Elizabeth Steiner Maccia, "Curriculum Theory and Policy," Bureau of Educational Research and Services, The Ohio State University, 1965, pp. 3-6.

18. A helpful discussion that is particularly relevant to the present investigation is in James Michael Lee, *The Flow of Religious Instruction*, pp. 39-43.

19. Fred N. Kerlinger, *Foundations of Behavioral Research* (New York: Holt, Rinehart and Winston, 1964), p. 11.

20. For example, Josef Andreas Jungmann, *Handing on the Faith: A Manual of Catechetics* (New York: Herder and Herder, 1962).

21. An example of this point of view is George Albert Coe, *A Social Theory of Religious Education* (New York: Scribner's, 1917). Also see Ernest J. Chave, *A Functional Approach to Religious Education* (Chicago: University of Chicago Press, 1947).

22. D. Campbell Wyckoff, *The Gospel and Christian Education*, p. 75.

23. James Michael Lee, Foreword, in James Michael Lee and Patrick C. Rooney, editors, *Toward a Future for Religious Education*, (Dayton, Ohio: Pflaum, 1970), p. 1.

24. Nicholas Lobkowicz, *Theory and Practice: History of a Concept from Aristotle to Marx* (Notre Dame, Indiana: University of Notre Dame Press, 1967), p. 31. Lobkowicz is a political scientist, but his discussion is particularly pertinent to this matter.

25. The application of theory in solving practical problems is among the behaviors that may be described as professional.

26. "Introductory," *Religious Education*, I (April, 1906), p. 1.

27. Charles F. Melchert, "Hope for the Profession," *Religious Education*, LXVII (September-October, 1972), p. 360.

28. *Ibid.*

29. D. Campbell Wyckoff, *The Gospel and Christian Education*, p. 78.

30. James Michael Lee, *The Flow of Religious Instruction*, p. 27.

31. *Ibid.*

32. Robert Boehlke, *Theories of Learning in Christian Education* (Philadelphia: Westminster, 1962), p. 17.

33. On this matter, see D. Campbell Wyckoff, *The Gospel and Christian Education*, pp. 72-81; and James Michael Lee, *The Flow of Religious Instruction*, pp. 39-43, 149-151.

34. Charles F. Melchert, "Hope for the Profession," p. 360.

35. James Michael Lee, *The Shape of Religious Instruction*, pp. 182-218; also relevant are pp. 133-176.

36. For a summary of the report of the Character Education Inquiry, see Hugh Hartshorne and Mark A. May, "A Summary of the Work of the Character Education Inquiry," *Religious Education*, XXV (September, 1930), pp. 607-619 and (October, 1930), pp. 754-762. This report was originally published by Macmillan in three volumes (1928, 1929, and 1930).

37. For an excellent translation of this treatise, see Aurelius Augustinus, *De Catechizandis Rudibus*, translated and edited by Joseph Patrick Christopher, The Catholic University of America Patristic Studies, Volume 8 (Washington, D.C.: The Catholic University of America, 1926).

38. Hugh Hartshorne and Mark A. May, "A Summary of the Work of the Character Education Inquiry" *Religious Education*, XXV (October, 1930), p. 756.

39. Andrè Godin, "Importance and Difficulty of Scientific Research in Religious Education: The Problem of the Criterion," *Religious Education*, LVII (May-June, 1962), p. 164.

40. *Ibid.*

41. See James Michael Lee, *The Flow of Religious Instruction*, p. 37.

42. Carter V. Good and Douglas E. Scates, *Methods of Research* (New York: Appleton-Century-Crofts, 1954), p. 279.

43. Robert Dubin, *Theory Building* (New York: The Free Press, 1969), p. 85.

44. Leonard A. Sibley, Jr., "Report of the Listening Team," *Religious Education*, LXII (September-October, 1967), pp. 428-430.

45. George A. Coe, *A Social Theory of Religious Education* (New York: Scribner's, 1917), pp. 9-10.

46. *Ibid.*

47. D. Campbell Wyckoff, "Toward a Definition of Religious Education as a Discipline," *Religious Education*, LXII (September-October, 1967), p. 393.

48. *Ibid.*, pp. 392-393.

49. *Ibid.*, p. 393.

50. Xavier James Harris, "The Development of the Theory of Religious Instruction in American Catholic Secondary Schools After 1920" (unpublished Ph.D. dissertation, University of Notre Dame, 1962), p. 26.

51. J. Gordon Chamberlin, *Freedom and Faith,* p. 23.

52. Nicholas Henry Beversluis, *Christian Philosophy of Education*, p. 15.

53. Lewis Joseph Sherrill, *The Rise of Christian Education* (New York: Macmillan, 1944), p. 2.

54. James Michael Lee, *The Flow of Religious Instruction*, p. 233.

55. Charles D. Hardie, *Truth & Fallacy in Educational Theory* (New York: Bureau of Publications, Teacher's College, Columbia University, 1962), p. 73.

56. Kendig Brubaker Cully, *The Search for a Christian Education–Since 1940* (Philadelphia: Westminster, 1965), p. 24.

57. William Bedford Williamson, *Language and Concepts in Christian Education.*

58. James Michael Lee, *The Flow of Religious Instruction*, pp. 18-19, and especially pp. 28-31.

59. Harrison S. Elliott, *Can Religious Education Be Christian?* (New York: Macmillan, 1940), pp. 1-11.

60. For example, James D. Smart, *Teaching Ministry of the Church*

(Philadelphia: Westminster, 1954), pp. 46-67, 61-63; also James Michael Lee, *The Shape of Religious Instruction*, p. 226.

61. Harrison S. Elliott, *Can Religious Education Be Christian?* pp. 1-11.

62. James Michael Lee and Patrick C. Rooney, editors, *Toward a Future for Religious Education.*

63. James Michael Lee, Foreword, in *ibid.*, p. 1.

Chapter II

The Traditional Theological Theoretical Approach to Religious Education

CRITERIA FOR THE TRADITIONAL APPROACH

The traditional theological approach to theorizing about religious education is delineated by the following criteria. *First,* theological conceptualizations, based upon data thought to be received by authoritative one-way revelation, are normative for all decisions relative to religious education theory and practice. The Bible is the only source of authoritative revelation for Protestant traditionalists while Roman Catholic traditional theorists include church tradition, which, with the Bible, is interpreted by the magisterium. *Second,* religious education is essentially concerned with the transmission of a unique, divinely authoritative, salvific message derived from the facts of revelation. *Third,* the religion teacher, who must first have received the unique salvific message and in some sense been commissioned to teach, is to transmit the divinely authoritative message fully and faithfully to students. An often used image of the religion teacher is that of a herald of good news. *Fourth,* students, following the reception of the authoritative message in its fullness, will live out the implications of the message both with respect to Christian living and eternal destiny.[1]

In addition to these criteria, it may be observed that typical representatives of the traditional theological approach are committed to a point of view which includes the dimension of the supernatural[2] as a major theoretical and practical issue for religious education. Teaching practices directly generated by the traditional approach tend to be verbal in nature, the lecture being their principal model.

ANTECEDENTS TO THE TRADITIONAL APPROACH

Augustine's *De Catechizandis Rudibus*,[3] one of the earliest extant major theoretical treatises on religious education from a Christian perspective, provides a convenient starting point for a brief survey of the antecedents to twentieth century traditional theorizing in regard to religious education. Deogratias, a frustrated religion teacher in Carthage near the beginning of the fifth century, apparently wrote to Augustine for suggestions on how to achieve more salutory results from his teaching. Augustine's reply to Deogratias, *De Catechizandis*, touches upon a number of significant theoretical issues, such as the problem of language, the teacher, the student, and the affective environment. The central concern of this early treatise, however, is clearly related to the communication of subject-matter content which Augustine locates almost exclusively in the Bible. *De Catechizandis* details several possibilities for arranging biblical materials in order that the subject matter considered by Augustine to be essential for complete instruction in the Christian faith will be covered according to the specific needs of students.

Augustine's theoretical notions as presented in *De Catechizandis Rudibus* have had a lasting influence upon subsequent religious educationists. The so-called Munich Method of religion teaching, for example, though acquiring its basic pedagogical framework from Herbartian teaching methods, nonetheless does insert a significant number of concepts derived from Augustine's reply to Deogratias.[4]

The religious educational theory expressed by Augustine in *De Catechizandis Rudibus* is typical of the implicit theory upon which the catechumenate,[5] the chief religious education endeavor of the early church, was based. After the demise of the catechumenate in the sixth and seventh centuries the church was largely without effective religious education activity until the period of the Reformation in the sixteenth century.[6]

Early in the sixteenth century, reacting to the energetic teaching of the Reformers, Roman Catholic leaders increased their efforts to promote the teaching of the Catholic religion. Catechism books, intended to present a clear and concise summary of the faith, were produced by both Protestants and

Catholics. Hence, the use of books written expressly to define and defend particular points of view came to dominate religious educational practice. The obvious theory upon which these book-oriented religious educational practices were founded was that *knowing the right answers* was the best way to live and to defend the Christian faith. Little was offered by way of change in either pedagogical theory or practice during the seventeenth and eighteenth centuries.[7]

Religion teaching during the nineteenth century reflected the influence of the enlightenment with its concentration upon reason as man's highest power. Rationalistic educational theories of the period, when applied to religious education, typically led to a line-by-line explanation of religion lessons by religion teachers and to rote memorization of lessons by students. By this time, in America, the Sunday school movement,[8] in which the Bible had replaced the catechism books, was in full bloom. During much of the nineteenth century, then, while Roman Catholic children under religious instruction were busy memorizing the lessons of the catechism, Protestant children in Sunday schools were busy memorizing the Bible. *When a child could repeat what was true and right, he would believe the truth and do the right thing as the Holy Spirit worked within him through the lessons that he had learned—or so the prevailing theory went.*

Protestant version of the traditional approach

The dawn of the twentieth century witnessed a series of significant changes in the approach to theory and practice which had characterized both Protestant and Catholic religious education during the nineteenth century. Within Protestantism, the Evangelical[9] cause which had supported and guided the Sunday school through its nineteenth century heyday was rendered increasingly rudderless by the emergence of changing religious and educational views. These new views, by incorporating liberal theology and progressive educational theories, gave rise to a perspective on religious education quite out of harmony with the Evangelical approach to religious education, committed as it was to the notion that the communication of a divinely ordained message was the most essential factor in religious education.[10]

The Protestant version of the traditional approach to religious education, dormant during the earlier decades of the twentieth century, experienced a reawakening in America partly as a result of the organization of the Evangelical Teacher Training Association in the 1930's. The founding of the National Association of Evangelicals (NAE) in 1942 provided additional encouragement to traditional religious educational thinking. The continuing commitment of the latter association has been to the orthodox doctrines of historic Protestantism, "doctrines that it finds in the Bible, received as the Book given throughout by inspiration."[11] The traditional educational leanings of Evangelicals continued to be expressed during the 1940's in a desire for a renewal of the vitality of the Sunday school along the lines of its earlier evangelically oriented form. These traditionalist sentiments eventuated in the establishment of the National Sunday School Association through the NAE's Church School Commission in 1946. A more-or-less official statement of the National Association of Evangelicals on matters of religious educational policy was made by Frank Gaebelein in *Christian Education in a Democracy.*[12] A striking example of the traditional theological mode of thought which characterizes the Evangelical position on religious education theory and practice, as reflected in *Christian Education in a Democracy,* is: "It is with this evangelical faith, not simply as another system of theology but as a unifying factor of Christian education, that this book is concerned. In a sense it is a summons to a position that is old and at the same time new. There are times when the only way to go forward is to go back. . . . And so, while our call to education is a call back to the Bible and Christ, it is at the same time a summons to go forward in Him."[13]

The National Association of Evangelicals has continued to provide a center of theological and educational identity for Evangelical Protestant religious educationists who typically approach theoretical and practical problems of religious education from a clearly traditional theological perspective which can be summarized as follows: (1) the Bible is the norm for religious educational theory and practice; (2) communication of the Gospel, as a message of salvation, is the central purpose of religious education; (3) the teacher is the human communicator who is supernaturally assisted by the Holy Spirit in the task of teaching religion; (4) the student, who receives the Gospel, is thereby affected both in time and eternity.

Roman Catholic version of the traditional approach

On the other side of the Atlantic, toward the end of the nineteenth century, the impact of the emerging science of psychology was beginning to be felt in educational circles particularly through the work of Johann Friedrich Herbart, a pioneer in the application of psychological principles to educational methodology. The Herbartian teaching method influenced the character of twentieth century religious education in the Roman Catholic Church through the modern catechetical renewal which began about 1900 in Munich, Germany. Heinrich Steiglitz, the early leader of the movement for catechetical renewal, developed a method of teaching religion which reflected the application of psychological principles as they were then understood. The religion teaching method developed by Steiglitz, sometimes referred to as the Munich Method, made use of the principles advanced by Herbart.[14]

The Munich Method and the theory upon which it was based exerted an expanding influence over religion teaching in the Roman Catholic Church in Europe during the early years of the twentieth century. The modern catechetical renewal, associated in the beginning with the Munich catechists under the leadership of Steiglitz, continues to influence—albeit, with waning force—a considerable number of Roman Catholic religious educationists and religion teachers in Europe. In a celebrated speech at the Eichstätt Conference on Catechetics (1960), Valerian Cardinal Gracias distinguished three stages that are descriptive of the way in which the catechetical renewal movement has maintained its influence by responding to changing times and situations: (1) the psychological stage, (2) the theological stage, and (3) the institutional stage.[15] The *psychological stage* was occupied during the earlier years of the twentieth century mainly with the previously mentioned problems of applying the then-current psychological theory to the teaching of religion.

The modern *theological stage* of the catechetical renewal was begun in 1936 through the publication of *Die Frohbotschaft und unsere Glaubensverkündigung*[16] by the Jesuit liturgist, Josef Jungmann. Jungmann longed for an infusion of the joyfulness of which he had seen glimpses in his liturgical studies of the early church. He called for a return to the supernatural element in religious education by insisting upon attention to content, principally the proclamation of a message—the core or center of which was Christ. Because of this emphasis upon the heralding of a message, the *kerygma,* the modern theological stage of the catechetical renewal has sometimes been called the "kerygmatic movement." Theorists commonly identified with the so-called kerygmatic movement in Roman Catholic religious education appear to be remarkably consistent in using the traditional theological approach to religious education; they hold that: (1) a theology grounded in the Bible and church tradition is the ultimate basis for all religious educational decisions, (2) the transmission of a unique, divinely ordained message is the primary task of religious education, (3) the teacher is a commissioned herald of the message, and (4) complete reception of the authoritative message will eventuate in Christian living and eternal felicity.

The *institutional stage* of the modern catechetical movement had its concretization in the post World War II development of such international organizations as the *Centre International D'études de la Formation Religieuse* ("Lumen Vitae") in Brussels and *The East Asian Pastoral Institute* in Manila. Traditional Catholic religious educationists have frequently worked in and through these institutional organizations to refine the theoretical underpinnings and practical expressions of the approach to religious education in the Catholic Church identified with the kerygmatic movement. The international journal, *Lumen Vitae,* published by the *Centre,* has been a major means of disseminating theoretical and practical notions characteristic of the kerygmatic movement—and thus, of the Roman Catholic version of the traditional theological theoretical approach to religious education as well.

REPRESENTATIVE TRADITIONAL THEORISTS

The analysis of the traditional theological theoretical approach to religious education in this chapter will be based upon an examination of pertinent books written by representative theorists selected from among Protestants associated with the

Evangelical movement,[17] and from among Roman Catholics associated with the kerygmatic movement. Religious educationists from these two Christian movements have engaged in possibly the most true-to-type traditional theological theorizing in the twentieth century. The similarity of language used by representative Protestant and Catholic traditionalists masks many significant nuances and outright differences in viewpoint; nonetheless, these theorists do appear to work from a single, identifiable, theoretical approach.

Representative Protestant theorists

One articulate Protestant traditional theorist is Frank Gaebelein. His major book touching upon religious educational theory is *Christian Education in a Democracy* (1951).[18] The theoretical position espoused by Gaebelein appears to fully meet the criteria for the traditional approach. The theoretical fundaments of his religious educational thought are doctrines found in the Bible. The heart of religious education, for Gaebelein, is the communication of biblical truths by teachers who are able to lead students to an understanding of these truths. He places a high priority on the verbal teaching of the scriptures and upon the pulpit as a functional center of Christian religious education.[19]

Lois LeBar, author of *Education That Is Christian* (1958),[20] is another Evangelical Protestant religious educationist who works out of a traditional approach. LeBar judges all matters of religious educational theory and practice upon the basis of fidelity to theological and biblical standards. She holds that all valid educational concepts are discoverable by Christian religious educationists who will look to the Creator of truth ("who has made the learner, his teacher, his content, and his environment") rather than to secular sources for information relative to religious education.[21] LeBar is sensitive to the potential vagaries of the lecture mode of teaching and is more visibly aware of the teaching-learning process than are many traditionalists; nevertheless, is an overall way she seems to maintain a consistent traditional theological point of view with respect to the theory and practice of religious education. Both teaching methods and the structure of the curriculum are derived by LeBar from the study of the Bible. She also places considerable emphasis upon the theory that the Holy Spirit, working through the teacher, actually accomplishes the aims of religious education.

Harold Carlton Mason, a longtime professor of religious education in such institutions of higher learning as Northern Baptist Seminary and Asbury Theological Seminary, is a third Evangelical Protestant who writes from a traditionalist approach to religious education. Mason, for whom Evangelical theology is normative for all aspects of religious education, is avowedly a transmissionist; he states: "Jesus said: 'I am the Way, the Truth and the Life.' This is an authoritative statement to be taught to children as final truth. There is more to Christian education than self-expression and activity from the evangelical point of view. In Christian education there is a body of knowledge to be transmitted, an ancient Book to be perpetuated."[22] Mason's two books, *Abiding Values in Christian Education* (1955)[23] and *The Teaching Task of the Local Church* (1959),[24] present something of a popularization of the traditional approach to the theory and practice of religious education.

Although Frank Gaebelein, Lois LeBar, and Harold Carlton Mason have been selected as the principal Protestant representatives of the traditional approach to religious education, other Evangelical Protestant religious educationists such as Clarence Benson, Peter Person, and C. B. Eavey write from a similar perspective. Their books will be used to provide necessary supplemental data on the Protestant traditional point of view.

Representative Catholic theorists

The theoretical stance of two influential European religious educationists, Josef Jungmann and Johannes Hofinger, seems to be well within the parameters of the traditional approach. Although Jungmann's 1936 book, *Die Frohbotshaft und unsere Glaubensverkündigung*,[25] was instrumental in bringing about a renewed interest in the communication of a biblically based message as a major concern in Roman Catholic religion teaching, his theoretical notions are more fully developed in a later book, *Handing on the Faith* (1962).[26] Even the title of this book is indicative of a traditional theoretical posture. Jungmann is insistent that the task of teaching religion involves the transference of doctrinal content by the joyous announcement of the kerygma after the manner that the apostles preached the Gospel in the early church—hence, the kerygmatic designation of the movement which follows upon Jungmann's work. Teaching practices closely related to Herbartian methods are advocated by Jungmann as being ideally suited to the faithful transmission of the Christian message.[27]

Johannes Hofinger, the author of numerous articles on religious educational themes in professional and popular publications, has advanced his theoretical and practical position most fully in *The Art of Teaching Christian Doctrine* (1962).[28] Theology is plainly preceptive in all theoretical and practical matters relative to religious education for Hofinger, as it is for Jungmann. For Hofinger, the work of the religion teacher, as a commissioned herald of the kerygma, is to proclaim Christ. He states: ". . . . Christ, the great Gift of the Father's love and our Way to the Father is Himself the central theme of our message. . . ."[29] A critical element in this theoretical viewpoint is that the totality of the Christian message, with its many dogmas and doctrines, must be fully proclaimed because it would be a "catechetical crime" to transmit to students only a fragment of the "organic divine message." Correct communication of the message, then, will result in religious living on the part of the student. Consistent with his theoretical approach, the religious educational practices proposed by Johannes Hofinger are mostly forms of the lecture.[30]

A third representative Catholic traditional theorist is Marcel van Caster whose principal theoretical work is *The Structure of Catechetics* (1965).[31] The theoretical notions posited in the *Structure of Catechetics* are extended into the dimension of religious educational practice in *Themes of Catechesis* (1966).[32] Religious educational theory and practice are based by van Caster in doctrines derived both from the Bible and from church tradition as interpreted by the magisterium. The aim of religion teaching, according to van Caster, is to faithfully transmit the word of God in such a way that it eventuates in "faith as knowledge" and contributes thereby to a "living faith." He is critical both of traditional transmissive and of "activist" modes of religion teaching. But his proposed synthesis, based upon "proclamation" and "interpretation" of the word of God, does not differ significantly from the verbal, lecture-oriented teaching techniques generated by the traditional theological approach to religious education.[33]

Other Roman Catholic religious educationists who have written books from a traditional theological approach include Josef Goldbrunner, Alphonso Nebreda, and G. Emmet Carter. Jungmann, Hofinger, and van Caster have been selected as the major Roman Catholic representatives of the traditional approach since their books seem to have had more theoretical and practical consequence than have the books of other "kerygmatic" religious educationists.

ANALYSIS OF THE TRADITIONAL APPROACH

The Aim

Genesis of aim

Theological considerations exert a determining influence on the aim of religious education for theorists of the traditional theological school of thought. Aim, for these theorists, is not a working construct to be changed as experience dictates; it is ultimately determined by divine purposes. Frank Gaebelein declares that while the goals of Christian education concern man and society, "the creative source of these goals is not within man and society. Rather it is implicit in a philosophy which . . . is derived neither from a sociological context nor from the pragmatic method but from revealed truth."[34] The Jesuit religious educationist, Marcel van Caster, dogmatically states that religious education's real purpose "is to communicate the word of God with a view to spreading the faith."[35] As is illustrated by van Caster's statement, *traditional theorists typically understand aim to be radicated in divine purposes in such a way that it may be achieved only through the communication of a divine message.* Johannes Hofinger simply says that the aim of teaching religion is "to convey the Christian message."[36]

Transmissive aspect of aim

Transmission of the Christian message comprises a key element in the aim of religious education for both Protestant and Catholic traditional theorists. One Protestant writer frankly states that the aim of religious education "involves transmissive teaching so much frowned upon by those whose views of democracy extend to freeing the child of any doctrinaire or imposed values as absolute. . . . In Christian education there is a body of knowledge to be transmitted. . . ."[37] A Catholic religious educationist reminds religion teachers not to lose sight of the fact that teaching religion means transferring the content of Christian doctrine to students.[38]

Supernatural element in aim

Traditional theorists are careful to specify that communicating the Christian message, though transmissive in function, is not to be equated with mere information transfer. Most traditionalists, accordingly, repudiate the rationalistically oriented theories which spawned the stereotyped rehearsal of doctrinal codes and rote memory methods which characterized religious education practices in the nineteenth century. Inclusion of the supernatural dimension in the communication of the Christian message, then, becomes a crucial theoretical element that marks the twentieth century traditional understanding of the aim of religious education (as compared with the nineteenth century rationalistically oriented theories).

Protestant traditionalists typically contrast *secular education* which is concerned only with life on the natural level with *Christian education* which recognizes man as more than a creature of this world. *Christian education* brings in the supernatural dimension in recognition of man's spiritual potentialities. Religious education, according to this viewpoint, should include the facilitation of a direct, experiential, present, and continuing encounter between the student and God through the communication of the divine message.[39] Frank Gaebelein, for instance, holds it to be the divine prerogative of the Sunday school to lead its students toward a vital experience with Christ and to train them to live in harmony with God.[40]

Roman Catholic traditional theorists, following Josef Jungmann's 1936 call for a revival of the "truly supernatural" by means of the joyous heralding of the "Good News proclaimed by Christ," also emphasize the supernatural element in their theorizing about religious educational aims. One representative theorist states that religious education must aim "to help bring about an encounter with the Lord."[41] Another traditionalist offers his opinion that religion teaching ought not impart only understanding about God, but it should also impart an "experience of God."[42] A third writer suggests that even though the religion teacher is engaging in a number of teaching activities he must always have in mind a single goal which is to help the student "open wide his heart to the activity of the Holy Spirit."[43] In *Handing on the Faith,* Jungmann himself declares that the religion teacher must "introduce the children to the supernatural world of faith in such a way that the momentous thoughts that are embraced by it become those ideals by which they can orient themselves and by which they can be guided on life's highway, and that these ideals evolve into powerful virtues which will propel them along the ways of Christian living."[44]

Knowledge of the faith and Christian living

The imparting of information is ordinarily considered by traditional theorists to be a necessary aim, though not a final goal of religious education. The character and quality of the student's life is the larger end toward which knowledge and understanding are contributory. This goal of lived religion is, in turn, intimately related to contact with the supernatural. *Traditional theological theorizing thus radicates Christian living on the part of the student in his reception of the Christian message and in the resultant work of the Holy Spirit through the message.* In a passage purporting to define the aims of the modern catechetical movement in Catholic religious education, Johannes Hofinger states: ". . . we not only have to give our students a thorough knowledge of their faith, but we must also form true Christians, who truly live their Christianity. Religious knowledge in itself is not the real goal of our teaching, it is only a means. The goal of religious instruction is religious living."[45] From the Protestant traditional perspective, a similar strong statement is made by C. B. Eavey in a monologue which details aims and objectives of Evangelical Christian education: "All that is done in Christian education has the one final aim of bringing those taught to perfection in Godly life and character."[46]

What traditional theorists mean by "religious living" and "a Godly life" is elaborated upon by two other representatives of this approach, Clarence Benson and Josef Jungmann. Benson proposes that the spiritual growth of the student in a religious educational setting should ideally result in a life in which there is (1) a place for worship and a continuing sense of fellowship with God, (2) right living through the development of Christian habits, and (3) a place of service both to man and God.[47] Jungmann also advances a comprehensive goal for Christian living: ". . . Christian culture will show signs of new life and become truly vigorous only when men bear the kingdom of God so enthusiastically within themselves that they will not have to await a command to carry it with them into their places of work, their recreation, their social life and their solitude."[48]

Concern for personal reception of the Christian message and for personal responsibility in living the Christian life has eventuated in a heightened interest in the individual student on the part of traditional theorists. This interest in the individual is illustrated in the literature by the use of singular terms such as "the child," "the student," or "the one who comes to be catechized." However, the initial assumptions of the traditionalist position have sometimes caused individual differences in particular pupils to be overlooked. Dissimilar characteristics of pupils often have been disregarded in the development of aims, especially those aims relating to religious living. Historically, within the Protestant Sunday school for example, Christian living was generally taken to be the natural by-product of the knowledge of the Bible and of a conversion experience. Teachers in Sunday schools usually worked under the impression (naturally deduced from transmissionist theory) that if they taught the outer facts of the Bible the Holy Spirit would do the necessary inner work to bring about the desired goals in the life of the individual pupils. Such teachers, according to Lois LeBar, "didn't consider it necessary for them to study human nature or to know the developmental stages through which pupils passed."[49] Johannes Hofinger describes a similar situation within the Roman Catholic religion teaching tradition, although he too suggests that religion teaching must continuously adapt itself to the child's psychology.[50] Nonetheless, the propensity of traditional theorists to state aims in terms of the reception of a unique message seems to make it difficult for them to be consistent in recognizing individual differences, in spite of their interest in individuals.

Scope of aim

The scope of the aim of religious education, from the traditional theological point of view, includes both right living in this present world and full participation in the eternal (supernatural) dimensions of God's kingdom. Protestant traditional theorists typically take a literal approach to this duality of religious educational aim. They see man as a creature of two worlds, related to the supernatural as well as to the natural realm, both of which must be included in the aim of religious education. Secular education—and much religious education—is charged by these religious educationists with being excessively preoccupied with proximate, natural goals. True *Christian education,* they hold, does not neglect this world, but looks in addition toward ultimate, eternal, supernatural goals—the personal knowledge of God and redemption through Christ.[51] Frank Gaebelein recognizes that this concentration upon ultimate goals raises the risk that the development of man in society may be overlooked. However, in the characteristic manner of other Protestant traditional theorists, he maintains that true morality rests first of all upon love of God and following this upon the love of men.[52]

Catholic traditional theorists also hold that the scope of religious educational aim should have both a present and an eternal dimension, but they do not force a separation upon these dimensions. Fulfillment of the full scope of religious education, according to these Catholic religious educationists, occurs naturally through full participation in the liturgical life and witness of the Catholic Church.

Use of aim in evaluation and the theoretical process

Insofar as it is a standard for determining the direction and extent of student progress in religious education settings, aim has received scant attention from traditional theorists. Two apparently related reasons for this scant attention are (1) that aims radicated in otherworldly, divine purposes are difficult to translate into meaningful, measurable phenomena, and (2) that aims stated by traditional theologically oriented theorists characteristically lack specificity.[53]

As a theoretical element in the traditional theological approach, aim does not seem to have contributed to any ongoing theoretical interaction whereby religious education practices may be significantly improved. To the contrary, the way in which traditional religious educationists have perceived the supernatural aspect of aim may well have desensitized them to the need for the development of more fruitful practices. A careful analysis of the writings of traditional theorists reveals a not uncommon attitude among them to be that any method will do because the Holy Spirit works over and above human practices in the accomplishment of God's purposes.[54]

The Content

The content of religious education, for theorists of the traditional school of thought, is an authoritative, biblically and theologically founded message to be given to students by a teacher who, having received the message and experienced its benefits, is a witness to it. The major source of content for these theorists is the Bible. The central theme of the religious message is the person, Christ.

Method — Content

Traditional theologically oriented religious educationists typically dichotomize the content of religious education and religion teaching method. Indeed, teaching method is often looked upon as merely subservient to the message (or content) of religious education. A representative Protestant theorist asserts: "Christian teaching realizes its responsibility for the proclamation of the gospel message, and therefore does not permit the message to be eclipsed by the method."[55] In similar fashion, a Roman Catholic religious educationist writes: "Rightly understood, methods of teaching are servants. They assist the teacher in making his teaching understood as accurately and as easily as possible. But methods must never be allowed to tyrannize over the meaning of what is taught."[56]

In accord with the prevailing conceptualizations among traditional theorists, this chapter will deal separately with *content* and *method,* even though some twentieth century religious educationists consider them to be of one piece.[57]

Biblical and doctrinal basis of authoritative content

The authoritative character of religious educational content, from the traditional viewpoint, is evident in the writings of both Protestant and Roman Catholic theorists. Protestant tradition- alists usually draw subject-matter content directly from the Bible, and they deduce the authority of the message from it as well. Catholic traditional theorists also derive subject-matter content mainly from the Bible, but they include the Catholic Church's magisterium as a source of authority for the message.

From the Protestant traditional perspective, religious educa- tion in the local church is built on the revelation of Jesus Christ in the Old and New Testament Scriptures. Consequently, Evan- gelical Protestants argue strongly for the use of the term, *Christian education,* because of what they consider to be its "distinctive content." Frank Gaebelein says of this matter: "Let it be said at once that the word 'Christian' is something more than a pious synonym for 'religious.' There are many religions; there is only one Christianity. The faith of the apostles and their successors through the ages is not just one among a number of world religions; instead, it is nothing less than the revelation of God to a lost world."[58]

As to the content of religious education, then, Protestant traditionalists are typically committed to the position that there is only one authentic and infallible source, the Bible. Thus, a Protestant traditionally oriented religious educationist pointed- ly affirms that the Bible is to be the text book for Christian teaching.[59]

It would be incorrect, however, to draw the conclusion that Protestant traditional theorists encourage no use of nonbiblical materials. Most such theorists suggest the use of other materials (hymns, history, social-problems, etc.). However, they strongly insist on a biblical core of subject-matter content and on a biblical interpretation of such other materials as are used. The message of the Gospel must, for their part, be preserved intact by a concentration upon biblical truth in the process of religious education.

From the Roman Catholic traditional perspective, the content of religious education is a revealed message of salvation which is not discoverable by man. This message, received by divine revelation, must be transmitted with authority under mandate from God: a mandate which is given to religion teachers through the bishop in behalf of the divine person, Jesus Christ—himself the focal point of the message.[60] Roman Catholic traditional theorists place more emphasis upon the church as a source of authority for religious educational content than do Protestants. Therefore, it is not surprising that one representative theorist should state that "God has provided certain guarantees within his Church. All religious instruction is imparted in accordance with the magisterium."[61] The same theorist also maintains that if the religion teacher teaches faithfully what the Catholic Church teaches, the content of his teaching will be something so vital that it will demand the adherence of the whole man.[62]

Still, Josef Jungmann suggests that the notion of authority relative to the content of religious education has to be adapted to new times. He notes that the complete and total submissiveness of an earlier Catholicism which entrusted itself to the motherly direction of the Catholic Church is no longer intact. Because of this, Jungmann holds that religion teaching cannot merely content itself with the bare handing on of hereditary formulas; rather, religion teaching must lead toward an "interior grasp" of the content of faith itself. According to this view, the content of religious education is to be identified with the "all embracing, salvific plan of God." The authority of this message, then, lies in the announcement (proclamation) of the facts concerning God's salvific intervention in history, the kerygma.[63]

The writings of Roman Catholic traditional theorists indicate that they rely as heavily upon the Bible for subject-matter content as do Protestant theorists. This biblical source of spirit and language, as well as of content, is evident in the following summary of the Christian message by the Jesuit religious educationist, Johannes Hofinger:

THIS IS THE MESSAGE WE PROCLAIM: In His infinite goodness, the Father in heaven has called us to be united with Him in life and joy, sharing His divine riches: through Christ, His Son—Him He gave as a ransom for us sinners, and into His likeness He desires that we be conformed, so that, born anew of water and of the Holy Spirit, and thus

made partakers of the divine nature, we may be children of
God. And because we are God's children, He has sent the
Spirit of His Son into our hearts: thus being the temple of
God, we are to live the life of God's children, following the
example of Christ, our first born brother, so that we may
gain the kingdom of God and His glory, as heirs of God,
joint heirs with Christ.[64]

Christ the central theme

The centrality of Jesus Christ is taken by traditional theologically oriented religious educationists to be the distinguishing
factor of the Christian religion. In turn, he is considered to be
the theme, the underlying principle, the heart of the content of
that religious education which enables students to live as
Christians.

*Above all, from the Protestant traditionalist theoretical position,
students must be introduced to the transcendent Christ,* since without a
vital contact with him no effective Christian religious education
is possible. Frank Gaebelein contends that: "The pupil must be
guided toward a crisis in his education that involves his repent-
ence, his unwithholding acceptance of Christ as his personal
Lord and Savior, his obedience, and his infilling by the Holy
Spirit."[65] Such an experience with Christ, according to Gaebelein, will produce a regenerated person and lay the foundation
for a Christian life, by enabling the student to conform to God's
will and grow toward Christian adulthood.[66] Lois LeBar proposes a religious educational paradigm in which both the living
Word (Christ) and the written Word (the Bible) are at the center
of the truly Christian curriculum.[67] Teaching religion, according to this paradigm, amounts to allowing the Bible, as em-
powered by the Holy Spirit, to change pupils according to God's
standards. Tests of effective teaching are made by measuring
growth and progress along the lines of the following goals: (1) to
lead students to Christ; (2) to build them up in Christ; and (3) to
send them out for Christ.[68]

*According to Roman Catholic traditionalist theorizing, the central
mystery to be proclaimed to the whole world is the message of the riches
that are in Christ.* This mystery of Christ is, accordingly, a
fundamental theme and unifying principle of traditionally

oriented Catholic religious education.[69] Focus on the person of the savior, from this viewpoint, should contribute to an easier and more lifegiving understanding of the distinctive content of the Christian message as well as to a more secure hold upon individual beliefs. Josef Jungmann, for example, states that: "The Mystical Christ sets forth most clearly the luminous center from which the whole of faith grows together into clear unity, since it is from the radiance of Christ that God's merciful plan, as well as its concrete realization, is rendered intelligible."[70] The duty of the religion teacher, then, is to proclaim the sacred message centered in Christ as clearly and meaningfully as possible, so that Christ shines forth as "the luminous core, who illumines every question, every doctrine, every command-ment."[71]

Transmission of content

The faithful transmission, or impartation, of an intact salvific message is the heart of religious education for most traditional theorists. This message (the content of religious education) is a matter of divine revelation and must be proclaimed as the word of God. Theology is considered by traditionalists to be fun-damental to the determination of the content which must be transmitted. One traditionalist believes that it is becoming in-creasingly evident that the most important and most authentic manifestation of God's word that is entrusted to the church is not the scientific elaboration but the transmission of the word by teaching in its several forms.[72] Another traditionalist holds that, since the aim of religious education is to shape the immortal destiny of the soul according to the word of God, the content of scripture must be imparted even before its principles are ap-plied.[73] Harold Carlton Mason maintains that the Christian message, which centers in Christ, is to be taught to students as final truth and that this involves the transmission of a body of content.[74] Josef Jungmann contends that teaching religion ne-cessitates transferring doctrinal content to students in fulfill-ment of their needs—needs which are basically spiritual in nature.[75]

The major currents of thought among traditionally oriented religious educationists continue to support the notion that the transmission of the unique Christian message will result in the desired cognitive, affective, and overt behaviors of students. However, some traditional thinkers are challenging the viability of the way that the traditional approach to religious education has relied almost exclusively upon verbal and cognitive formulations of the Christian message. Marcel van Caster, for instance, remarks upon the language problems involved in transmitting certain aspects of religious truth through words alone.[76] Lois LeBar laments the fact that through the years Sunday school teachers have relied so heavily upon verbal communication of facts in religion teaching. This communication has been assessed in most Sunday schools, according to LeBar, only by the ability of the student to repeat this outer knowledge verbally rather than by other evaluative measures which might have touched upon life-style or attitudes. She remarks, somewhat acerbically, that in Christian circles we have been content to point to a person and say, "He knows better than that; why does he do it?"[77]

Arrangement of content

The arrangement of subject-matter content to maximize the likelihood of clear transmission of the Christian message is a prime concern for traditional theological theorists. The most common characteristic of plans offered for this purpose is a concentration upon the biblical narrative as the framework for ordering religious education content. Within this biblical framework, the economy of salvation centered in an understanding of the person and work of Christ typically provides a unifying theme. Even the actual outline arrangement is thought by some traditionalists to be a theological rather than an educational topic. It would be misleading to imply that other factors affecting the organization of content are neglected by traditional theorists. These other factors, though, are generally looked upon simply as potential aids to a better theological solution to the problem of arranging the subject-matter content in order to effect the faithful transmission of the message. Johannes Hofinger offers a typical traditional rationale for a full and complete ordering of content in a plan for presentation: "We heralds have no right to be careless with these riches given us, nor to transmit to our charges only certain fragments of the whole message."[78] Similarly, Clarence Benson avers that the

Sunday school simply cannot fulfill the requirements of the task committed to it unless the content peculiar to its responsibilities, the gospel message, is arranged in a consecutive, comprehensive, and complete plan.[79]

The Teacher

The religion teacher, as the agent who transmits the Christian message, is the central human instrument in the religious educational endeavor according to typical formulations of the traditional approach to religious education. Hence, according to this approach, religion teachers must be selected with consummate care from among those prospects who first of all have the necessary religious and personal qualifications to fit them for this distinctive task.

The teacher's religious qualifications

Both Protestant and Roman Catholic traditional theorists specify that the religion teacher must be a member of "the faith" (as "the faith" is defined by the particular theorist). Thus, one Protestant traditionalist maintains that only the teacher who has been "made a new creature in Christ" is able to nurture others in the Christian faith.[80] Frank Gaebelein contends that the qualification of "newness of life through faith in the savior" is so essential for teaching in a Christian educational setting that it must never be waived.[81] From a Roman Catholic viewpoint, G. Emmett Carter suggests that the life-giving truth of Christ reaches students only through the ministrations of the Catholic teacher who is an instrument of God and of the Catholic Church.[82] Protestant traditional theorists make little distinction, so far as religion teaching is concerned, between ordained and lay teachers; they hold that (in view of the stupendous nature of the task) ministers and laymen, professionally trained educators and volunteer workers must work side by side in the teaching ministry of the local church.[83] Roman Catholic theorists strongly prefer that priests teach in religious educational situations whenever possible. For example, Josef Jungmann contends that priests should normally perform the religion teaching function since: "Granted equal pedagogical ability the priest catechist will always be more highly esteemed than other catechists."[84] When necessary, the use of other teachers including lay teachers is encouraged with the provision, however, that they stress the role and authority of the ordained priest and manifest a "genuine Catholic subordination and harmonious collaboration with him."[85]

The teacher's personal qualifications

In addition to the initial religious qualifications, traditional theorists have suggested a broad range of complementary personal requisites for the religion teacher. *Authentic Christian character* is considered by some traditional theorists to be the first personal requisite for a religion teacher. The religion teacher, according to these theorists, must live in witness to the message that he proclaims. Lois LeBar argues that it will do little good to refine teaching procedures if the teacher's life does not correspond to his words.[86] Other traditional theorists make *personality* the prime factor contributing to successful religion teaching. Thus, Josef Jungmann quotes Michael Phiegler with approval: "The religion teacher will succeed in teaching to that extent to which he himself has advanced as a personality."[87] *A commission or call* is assumed by most traditional theorists to be a necessary requisite for teaching religion. One Protestant theorist says that without a call no other capacities will make a Christian teacher worthy of the name.[88] From the Catholic perspective, a traditional theorist proposes that when a religion teacher is commissioned by ecclesiastical superiors, he is sent out to teach by Christ himself.[89] Both Protestant and Catholic traditionalists theorize that *a holy zeal for the kingdom of God* is a requirement for teaching religion effectively.[90]

Fidelity to the message is another requisite held necessary by many traditional theorists, both Protestant and Catholic. Johannes Hofinger says that fidelity to the message is the most important virtue of the herald of Christ's message, a virtue which causes him to proclaim his message exactly, carefully, and diligently.[91] Still other requisites for the teacher of religion that have been mentioned by traditional theorists are: *a sense of prayer*, without which the teacher will accomplish nothing by way of communicating his faith to others;[92] *unselfishness*, perfect accomplishment of Christ's commission is said to leave no time or interest for oneself;[93] and "*brains*," because mediocre efforts on the part of religion teachers imply that Christianity stands for second best.[94]

The teacher's training

The theoretical issues involved in training religion teachers are perceived in much the same way by Protestant and Roman Catholic traditionally oriented religious educationists. They insist that the most necessary competencies of religion teachers are rooted in and nurtured by the previously discussed religious and personal characteristics. Nevertheless, there is strong support among them for some sort of a program to prepare prospective teachers and to update the teaching skills of teachers in service.

Training programs for religion teachers proposed by both Protestant and Catholic traditionalists are highly reflective of the traditional theoretical focus upon the communication of a divinely revealed salvific message as the major responsibility of religious education. Accordingly, such programs usually concentrate upon *the faithful understanding of the message* as the most essential element in any training program. To this end, Protestants typically advocate Bible studies while Catholics recommend doctrinal studies as the heart of the program. All other elements in traditionally oriented teacher training programs theoretically contribute to the capacity of the teacher to transmit the content of the message to students.

Protestant traditional theorists usually have the teaching staff of the Sunday school in mind when they speak of training teachers. In this instance, the teachers are almost always lay volunteers. D. K. Reisinger charges that teachers in Sunday schools typically (1) lack formal training, (2) have little knowledge of the Sunday school textbook, the Bible, (3) may be quite unaware of effective teaching methods, and (4) are often indifferent in their attitude. Most Evangelical Protestant teachers, he says, confess that God and the Bible are important, but what they believe (and say) may be entirely different from what they teach. Consequently, the students, by observing the nonverbal communication of the teacher, may in fact learn that the sacred truths spoken in Sunday school are really not as important as the secular truths taught by superior teachers in public school.[95]

Clarence Benson, an originator of the Evangelical Teacher Training Association in the 1930's, maintains that such problems as those mentioned by Reisinger, are best solved by teacher training that anticipates and prevents Sunday school problems arising from incompetent teaching.[96] Benson contends that success in teaching can be assured to all who will be guided by the recognized principles of pedagogy; he is also careful to intimate that these principles do not conflict with the work of the Holy Spirit.[97]

The format of teacher-training programs typically advocated by Protestant traditional theorists includes: (1) *the study of the Bible* and related subjects such as doctrine, historical geography, and antiquities; (2) *the study of the pupil* and his psychology; and (3) *training in techniques and methods of teaching.* (Some Protestant traditional theorists consider mastery of the Bible to be the most essential foundation for teaching, not only because it is the "text book" but because it is also thought to be the best source of information about the pupil and about teaching method.)[98]

Roman Catholic traditional theorists concern themselves with (1) the training of priests, (2) the training of other religious,[99] and (3) the training of lay religion teachers. Each of these categories presents, for them, somewhat different theoretical problems. Jungmann argues, for example, that every priest and religious possesses the basic talents required for teaching religion.[100] By and large, religion teacher training programs proposed by Roman Catholic traditional theorists place their emphasis in three areas: *first,* the understanding of the content of the divinely revealed message through the appropriate study of Christian doctrine, the Holy Bible, the liturgy, and other contributory topics (religious, and most especially priests, are presumed to fulfill this and the following requirement in their normal studies); *second,* the personal development of the religion teacher through stress upon spiritual formation, character training, and social behavior in order that he may be "a good witness to Christ"; and *third,* the acquisition of skills and methods deemed appropriate to the sacred task of teaching religion (which task, though perceived to be ultimately a matter of divine grace, must make use of human resources, i.e. methods).[101]

The teacher's method

Traditional theologically oriented religious educationists typically understand teaching method to be a means to an end (i.e. the faithful communication of the Christian message to students). There is little commitment, ultimately, to a particular method since one method is reputed to be quite as good as another so long as it helps convey the Christian message to students. The teaching method advanced by Johann Friedrich Herbart during the nineteenth century, however, has profoundly influenced twentieth century teaching practices in both Protestant and Catholic religious educational settings. The Herbartian method (popularly formulated in five so-called "formal steps": preparation, presentation, association, generalization, and application) affected the methodological thinking of some Evangelical Protestant religious educationists, and its concepts were used in the development of the Munich Method of religion teaching. The Herbartian teaching method, oriented as it was toward the communication of ideas in a clear and complete way, appealed to religious educationists concerned with the orderly transmission of a divinely ordained message as the means whereby both desired behaviors and the salvation of students might be effected.

Roman Catholic traditional theorists make more use of methodological concepts directly related to Herbartian theory than do Protestant theorists. The overarching teaching method, as distinguished from teaching techniques, advocated by most Catholic traditionalists is derived directly from the Munich Method. Josef Jungmann's discussion of teaching method in *Handing on the Faith* indicates his conviction that this method, which he calls the "text-developing method," is the most reliable one for teaching religion because of its capacity to convey subject-matter content. Jungmann believes it is the preeminent teaching method, the method used by Christ himself. He objects to the exclusive identification of the text-developing method with Herbart's notions. "Vitalization" of the text-developing, or Munich Method (the five steps of which are preparation, presentation, explanation, summary, and application) may be accomplished, according to Jungmann, through the judicious use

of "the activity principle" and "the personal experience principle."[102] Johannes Hofinger, who contends that teaching method exists primarily to serve the teacher in communicating his
message, similarly sets forth an overall teaching method which
closely resembles the Munich Method with its Herbartian
framework. He distinguishes three stages of learning (perception, assimilation, and response) as a "basic law" to which
correspond three stages, or steps, in the process of teaching
(presentation, explanation, and application). Hofinger believes
that this method is "based on God's way of winning men" rather
than upon mere psychological theories.[103]

The teaching method advanced by post-Jungmann Roman
Catholic traditional theorists usually unfolds through the narra-
tion of salvation history. According to most of these theorists,
the biblical narrative provides the theologically and psychologically soundest, as well as the simplest and most effective means
of initiation into the Christian religion.[104] It should also be
noted that the religion teacher's life is considered by Catholic
traditional theorists to be generative of the teaching method
which he outwardly employs. Thus, Marcel van Caster can
remark: "We must be excused for insisting on this, but in our
opinion, the spirit of the teaching is far more important than the
technique. More than skill, it is the mentality of the teacher
which influences his pupils. It is his mentality based on his deep
knowledge of the Christian faith which forms conscious
Christians."[105]

A striking aspect of the Protestant traditional treatment of
teaching method is the eclectic manner in which teaching methods are proposed for use by religion teachers. Some of these
writers assume that since all students (and all lesson content)
cannot be taught in the same way, the teacher should therefore
be taught competencies in a number of methods (better termed
"techniques") such as storytelling, recitation, discussion, lecture, and the like. These "methods" are to be used as deemed
appropriate by the teacher. Another opinion is that teachers of
young children should have a flair for the dramatic and be
adept storytellers while teachers of adults should be able to use
discussion and lecture as the preferred methods. No single
teaching method seems to have been adopted as a model by
Protestant traditional theorists in the way that the Munich

Method has been adopted by Catholic traditional theorists. Frank Gaebelein observes that there is much work yet to be done in integrating the teaching methodologies employed in schools operating within the Evangelical Protestant tradition.[106] Lois LeBar charges that many Sunday school teachers use a method (blamed on an earlier Herbartian influence) that can only be described as "poor lay preaching."[107] Harold Carlton Mason regards it as unfortunate that the commitment to "transmissive teaching" (of which he approves) has led to a dependency on stereotyped verbal teaching methods. He believes that "transmissive teaching" is capable of adopting many methods and techniques to its purposes.[108]

Lois LeBar has attempted to develop a comprehensive teaching method through a theoretical process consistent with the traditional theological approach to religious education. She surmises that a chief reason for the lack of life and vitality in much Evangelical Protestant religion teaching is that teaching methods derived from a number of "man-made systems" have been used. The distinctive content of the Christian revelation, she contends, calls for distinctive treatment. Consequently, a better approach to teaching method would be to discover "God's system" and to develop teaching methods from it. LeBar's book, *Education That Is Christian,* amounts to a search for "God's system" through the analysis of teaching methods used by biblical personalities, particularly the method used by Jesus, "the Teacher come from God." Since Jesus did not use stereotyped methods, LeBar concludes that the "scriptural method" is not a stereotyped method. She develops a curriculum plan for teaching religion in which the Word of God, both living (Christ) and written (the Bible), is at the center. The appropriate teaching method for this curriculum makes use of such concepts as pupil needs, life situations, personal experiences, and most especially, the Holy Spirit. In fact, according to LeBar, this "scriptural method" eventuates in the human teacher working harmoniously with the Divine teacher, the Holy Spirit. In summary of her approach to teaching method, LeBar states: "The problem is to find God's ways of working, and work with Him, not to try to wheedle God into blessing our schemes. Since Christian teaching may be defined as discovering God's ways of working and working with Him, we need to learn by Scripture and by experience all God wants us to know of the ways of His Spirit. Not that we should try to unscrew the inscrutable, but these things which God has revealed belong to us and to our children (Deuteronomy 29:29)."[109]

As is true of Roman Catholic traditional theorists, Protestant traditionalists typically hold that, over and above any use of teaching method, the teacher's personal life and Christian witness is foundational to religion teaching success. "The person himself," according to LeBar, "is the key to spiritual ministry; we are our own chief method."[110]

The Student

The student in a religious educational setting, from the traditional theological viewpoint, is to be the recipient of an authoritative, divinely ordained, salvific message. Student variables (such as how the student learns, developmental differences, and the like) are of theoretical interest to traditionally oriented religious educationists essentially because of the possibility that such information may enable the message to be more effectively communicated to the student. This attitude toward the student is succinctly stated from the Protestant perspective by Donald Joy: "Man is a specially endowed creature with a capacity to know and to learn; if he is to be well served by the church, we must be attentive to the ways of knowing and to the emerging strategies of learning so as to help human beings grasp the vision of themselves and their world which is the distinctive property of the Christian faith."[111] From the Catholic perspective, Josef Jungmann notes: "As catechists, we must as a consequence present Christian doctrine in such a way that it is grasped by the child. To this end we must take into account their psychological differences, especially those special peculiarities of disposition, which are relevant to their religious training."[112]

Possibly the one characteristic of the student which is most crucial to traditional theorizing about religious education is that he is assumed to participate in the supernatural as well as the natural order. The central religious educational process (though affected by the natural dimension of existence) is considered to be, at its core, a supernatural process. Evangelical Protestants, then, typically look upon the student as God's creation, made in God's image, but with this image distorted through sin and therefore in need of supernatural renewal.[113] Roman Catholics see the student (providing he has been baptized) as not merely a natural being, but as a creature who belongs to the supernatural order through sanctifying grace; the largely unconscious supernatural life of the student needs to be developed and brought to consciousness by religious education.[114] For both Protestants and Catholics, it is through the communication (transmission) of the Christian message that the supernatural core-process of religious education is effected, at least theoretically.

Protestant traditional theorists usually agree that the student deserves to be considered in theorizing about the religious educational process. After all, as one traditionally oriented writer puts it, even church-related schools are not ends in themselves since they exist for the sake of the pupils in whose life the goals of education are to be realized.[115] Another writer suggests that students ought to have a place in the theoretical process because it is they who "must have dealings with the Lord."[116] However, even though Protestant traditional theorists do give some consideration to the student and to the teaching-learning process, they appear to place little reliance upon these factors in their actual theorizing. Lois LeBar writes: "the important thing is what is happening inside the pupil. . . . We teachers can influence these inner factors only by manipulating the outer. . . . Modern man cannot hope to improve upon the concept of teaching that the Lord God Himself has given in John 16:13. Because the Holy Spirit is the only Teacher who is able to work both inside and outside the pupil."[117] Frank Gaebelein expresses the philosophical and theological underpinnings of this distrust of pedagogical practices based upon studies of the student; he remarks: "Since man is in reality a creature of two worlds and possesses spiritual capacity and eternal destiny, the present provides no adequate basis for his education."[118]

Catholic traditional theorists likewise have a theological and philosophical view of man which causes them to consider the student in a religious educational setting to be mainly the receiver of a message. Given this theological view of religious education the theoretical problem for both Protestant and

Catholic traditional writers is to ascertain how the divinely ordained message might best be communicated to the student.

The Environment

As a usable variable in day-to-day religious educational practice environment is largely ignored by traditionally oriented theorists. Despite the fact that these persons acknowledge certain environmental effects they appear to be committed to a viewpoint which ultimately attributes behavior (overt or otherwise) to intellectual and other inner "spiritual" factors. Thus, one traditionalist maintains that students themselves determine their behaviors, notwithstanding their continual interaction with the environment.[119] In a similar vein, another theorist suggests that clear mental possession of the details of the Christian faith should provide a bulwark against a hostile environment.[120]

Among traditional theorists, particularly Catholics, recognition is given to the home, the school, and the parish church as environmental components which contribute to religious education. However, these components are considered more or less adjuncts to the "real" (i.e. content-oriented) religious educational process and are not integrated into religious educational theory and practice in a dynamic way. In fact, the establishment of Christian schools[121] may be looked upon as an attempt to ameliorate, rather than to actually use, environmental effects—especially since the environment is typically perceived to be unfriendly to Christian values. This mentality seems to militate against the use of environmental variables in day-to-day religion teaching because of the possible contamination, or dilution, of the Christian message.

The modified, overall environment of the typical Christian school, then, supposedly affords students the opportunity to gain intellectual strength and to tighten their grasp upon the Christian message so that, as a result, they will be enabled to "live the Christian life" when they "go out into the world." Frank Gaebelein argues that it may be put down as a cardinal biblical principle that the Christian is not at home in the world, that there is always a tension between the Christian and the environment (i.e. world) which can never provide an adequate basis for his education.[122] Josef Jungmann similarly contends that Catholics ought to resist the influence of the hostile world by creating another kind of world within the school and its religious life.[123]

Evaluation

Evaluation of student learning outcomes (whether of knowledge, attitude, belief, or overt behavior) plays little part in traditional theorizing about religious education. One probable reason for this is that traditionalists do not necessarily expect demonstrable effects of the Christian message to follow immediately upon its reception by students. A careful reading of the books of traditional theorists reveals a not uncommon attitude among them to be that: "The truth of God, faithfully taught, often works by delayed action."[124] Hence, the teacher (and the content of his lesson) rather than the student (and his learning outcomes) is the most crucial focus of evaluation from the traditional theoretical perspective.[125]

Notes for Chapter II

1. The hypothetical criteria used to delineate the four selected theoretical approaches are derived from an examination of religious educational literature. An extended investigation of these approaches to determine their full scope and character, though beyond the limitations of time and space allowed the present writer, is of such significance to the field of religious education that another investigator may well wish to pursue this matter. The present investigation is limited to an exploration of the consequences of these four approaches with respect to the six investigative categories.

2. "Supernatural" is a term which has acquired many nuances of meaning. Of particular relevance to this chapter is Ernst Niermann's comment to the effect that supernatural trends are most evident among Protestants concerned with preserving the supernatural character of biblical revelation and among Catholic traditionalists desiring a guaranteed, authoritative, divine revelation. See Ernst Niermann, "Supernaturalism" in *Sacramentum Mundi: An Encyclopedia of Theology,* edited by Karl Rahner (6 volumes; New York: Herder and Herder, 1970) VI, p. 191. For a more extended discussion of the natural and the supernatural in relation to religious education, see James Michael

Lee, *The Flow of Religious Instruction* (Dayton, Ohio: Pflaum/Standard, 1973), pp. 258-293.

3. See Aurelius Augustinus, *De Catechizandis Rudibus,* translated and edited by Joseph Patrick Christopher, The Catholic University of America Patristic Studies, Volume 8 (Washington, D.C.: The Catholic University of America, 1926).

4. "The Munich Method bears on its form and features unmistakable signs of relationship to *De Catechizandis Rudibus.*" John T. McMahon, *Some Methods of Teaching Religion* (London: Burns, Oates & Washburn, 1928), p. 1.

5. For a brief discussion of the catechumenate, see Lewis Joseph Sherrill, *The Rise of Christian Education* (New York: Macmillan, 1944), pp. 186-197.

6. See Gerard S. Sloyan, "The Relation of the Catechism to the Work of Religious Formation," in Gerard S. Sloyan, editor, *Modern Catechetics: Message and Method in Religious Formation* (New York: Macmillan, 1963), p. 95.

7. Josef Andreas Jungmann, *Handing on the Faith: A Manual of Catechetics* (New York: Herder and Herder, 1962), pp. 19-26.

8. The modern Sunday school movement is said to have begun in 1780 in Glouster, England when Robert Raikes gathered children from the streets of the city to study on Sundays; it found its "full flower" in nineteenth century America. For a readable history of the Sunday school, see Robert Wood Lynn and Elliott Wright, *The Big Little School: Sunday Child of American Protestantism* (New York: Harper & Row, 1971).

9. "Evangelical," as used in this work, is not a denominational term; rather, it designates a point of view which emphasizes the authority of the scriptures. "Evangelicals" typically accept the formulations of doctrine common to all orthodox sections of Protestantism, and they usually stress the importance of a personal reconciliation to God through Christ. See Frank E. Gaebelein, *Christian Education in a Democracy* (New York: Oxford, 1951), pp. 15-17; and Kendig Brubaker Cully, *The Search for a Christian Education–Since 1940,* (Philadelphia: Westminster, 1965), pp. 94-99.

10. Harold Carlton Mason, "The History of Christian Education," in J. Edward Hakes, editor, *An Introduction to Evangelical Christian Education* (Chicago: Moody Press, 1964), especially, pp. 31-33. A different perspective may be seen in William Clayton Bower and Percy Roy Hayward, *Protestantism Faces Its Educational Task Together* (Appleton, Wisconsin: Nelson, 1949), pp. 1-65.

11. Frank E. Gaebelein, *Christian Education in a Democracy,* p. 15.

12. *Ibid.*

13. *Ibid.*, pp. 16-17.

14. Herbartian theory assumes that knowledge of content is automatically transferred into feeling, willing, and doing. See John T. McMahon, *Some Methods of Teaching Religion*, pp. 1-25; and Klemens Tilman, "Origin and Development of Modern Catechetical Methods," in Johannes Hofinger, editor, *Teaching All Nations*, revised and partly translated by Clifford Howell (New York: Herder and Herder, 1961), pp. 81-94.

15. Valerian Cardinal Gracias, "Modern Catechetical Renewal and the Missions," in Johannes Hofinger, editor, *Teaching All Nations*, revised and partly translated by Clifford Howell (New York: Herder and Herder, 1961), especially pp. 11-14.

16. The most accessible version for English readers is Josef Andreas Jungmann, *The Good News Yesterday and Today*, translated (abridged) and edited by William A. Huesman (New York: Sadlier, 1962). This book is the twenty-fifth anniversary edition of Jungmann's *Die Frohbotschaft und unsere Glaubensverkündigung*. It also includes four essays in appraisal of the original work.

17. The National Association of Evangelicals (NAE) is a convenient point of reference for the Evangelical movement.

18. Frank E. Gaebelein, *Christian Education in a Democracy* (New York: Oxford, 1951). This book appears to substantially represent Gaebelein's personal position, even though its genesis was a charge to an NAE committee. See Kendig Brubaker Cully, *The Search for a Christian Education—Since 1940*, p. 103.

19. Frank E. Gaebelein, *Christian Education in a Democracy*, especially pp. 227-235.

20. Lois E. LeBar, *Education That Is Christian* (Old Tappan, New Jersey: Revell, 1958).

21. *Ibid.*, pp. 49-52, 135-168, 229-245.

22. Harold Carlton Mason, *The Teaching Task of the Local Church* (Winona Lake, Indiana: Light and Life, 1960), p. 25.

23. Harold Carlton Mason, *Abiding Values in Christian Education* (Westwood, New Jersey: Revell, 1955).

24. Harold Carlton Mason, *The Teaching Task of the Local Church* (Winona Lake, Indiana: Life and Life, 1960).

25. Josef Andreas Jungmann, *Die Frohbotschaft und unsere Glaubensverkündigung* (Regensburg: Pustet, 1936).

26. Josef Andreas Jungmann, *Handing on the Faith: A Manual of Catechetics*, translated and revised by A. N. Fuerst (New York: Herder and Herder, 1962).

27. *Ibid.*, pp. 65-221.

28. Johannes Hofinger, *The Art of Teaching Christian Doctrine* (Notre Dame, Indiana: University of Notre Dame Press, 1962).

29. *Ibid.*, p. 9.

30. *Ibid.*, pp. 10-89.

31. Marcel van Caster, *The Structure of Catechetics* (New York: Herder and Herder, 1965).

32. Marcel van Caster, *Themes of Catechesis* (New York: Herder and Herder, 1966).

33. Marcel van Caster, *The Structure of Catechetics*, pp. 7-21, 169-181.

34. Frank E. Gaebelein, *Christian Education in a Democracy*, p. 259.

35. Marcel van Caster, *The Structure of Catechetics*, p. 13.

36. Johannes Hofinger, *The Art of Teaching Christian Doctrine*, p. 65.

37. Harold Carlton Mason, *The Teaching Task of the Local Church*, p. 25.

38. Josef Andreas Jungmann, *Handing on the Faith*, p. xii.

39. Harold Carlton Mason, *Abiding Values in Christian Education*, pp. 15-33; also Lois E. LeBar, *Education That Is Christian*, pp. 135-168.

40. Frank E. Gaebelein, *Christian Education in a Democracy*, p. 227.

41. Marcel van Caster, *Themes of Catechesis*, p. 203.

42. Josef Goldbrunner, "Catechesis and Encounter," in Joseph Goldbrunner, editor, *New Catechetical Methods*, translated by M. Veronica Riedl (Notre Dame, Indiana: University of Notre Dame Press, 1965), p. 22.

43. Johannes Hofinger, "Appendices," in *Teaching All Nations*, p. 403.

44. Josef Andreas Jungmann, *Handing on the Faith*, p. 94.

45. Johannes Hofinger, *The Art of Teaching Christian Doctrine*, p. 17.

46. C. B. Eavey, "Aims and Objectives of Christian Eudcation," in *An Introduction to Evangelical Christian Education*, p. 62.

47. Clarence H. Benson, *The Christian Teacher* (Chicago: Moody Press, 1950), pp. 87-89.

48. Josef Andreas Jungmann, *The Good News Yesterday and Today*, p. 166.

49. Lois E. LeBar, *Education That Is Christian*, pp. 27-30.

50. Johannes Hofinger, *The Art of Teaching Christian Doctrine*, pp. 1-3.

51. Harold Carlton Mason, *The Teaching Task of the Local Church*, p. 12, and Frank E. Gaebelein, *Christian Education in a Democracy*, pp. 260-262.

52. Frank E. Gaebelein, *Christian Education in a Democracy*, p. 261.

53. Though one traditionalist postulates that aim makes measurement possible by providing a basis for determining how well religion teaching has progressed, it is difficult to see how the following aim may be measured (no matter how desirable): " . . . to shape the immortal destiny of a soul according to the Word of God." Clarence H. Benson, *The Christian Teacher*, pp. 79, 221-223.

54. Johannes Hofinger, *The Art of Teaching Christian Doctrine*, pp. 62-65.

55. Clarence H. Benson, *The Christian Teacher*, p. 14.

56. Johannes Hofinger, *The Art of Teaching Christian Doctrine*, pp. 12-13.

57. See James Michael Lee, *The Flow of Religious Instruction*, p. 19.

58. Frank E. Gaebelein, *Christian Education in a Democracy*, pp. 13-14.

59. C. B. Eavey, *Principles of Teaching for Christian Teachers* (Grand Rapids, Michigan: Zondervan, 1940), p. 13.

60. Josef Goldbrunner, "Catechetical Method as Handmaid of Kerygma," in *Teaching All Nations*, especially pp. 112-118.

61. Marcel van Caster, *Themes of Catechesis*, p. 205.

62. Marcel van Caster, "The Spirit of the Religion Course," *Lumen Vitae*, VI (July-September, 1951), pp. 438-439.

63. Josef Andreas Jungmann, *Announcing the Word of God*, translated by Ronald Walls (London: Burns & Oates, 1967), pp. 59-60; also Josef Andreas Jungmann, *The Good News Yesterday and Today*, especially pp. 7-8.

64. Johannes Hofinger, *The Art of Teaching Christian Doctrine*, p. 92.

65. Frank E. Gaebelein, *Christian Education in a Democracy*, p. 229.

66. *Ibid.*

67. Lois E. LeBar, *Education That Is Christian*, pp. 203-207.

68. Lois E. LeBar, *Children in the Bible School* (Westwood, New Jersey: Revell, 1952), pp. 193-194.

69. Johannes Hofinger, *The Art of Teaching Christian Doctrine*, p. 11.

70. Josef Andreas Jungmann, *The Good News Yesterday and Today*, p. 9.

71. *Ibid.*, p. 11.

72. Josef Andreas Jungmann, *Announcing the Word of God*, p. 28.

73. Clarence H. Benson, *The Christian Teacher*, p. 223.

74. Harold Carlton Mason, *The Teaching Task of the Local Church*, p. 25.

75. Josef Andreas Jungmann, *Handing on the Faith*, p. xii.

76. See Marcel van Caster, *Themes of Catechesis*, pp. 203-207; also *The Structure of Catechetics*, especially pp. 168-214.

77. Lois E. LeBar, *Education That Is Christian*, p. 30.

78. Johannes Hofinger, *The Art of Teaching Christian Doctrine*, p. 51.

79. Clarence H. Benson, *The Sunday School in Action* (Chicago: Moody Press, 1952), p. 138.

80. C. B. Eavey, "Aims and Objectives of Christian Education," in *An Introduction to Evangelical Christian Education*, p. 61.

81. Frank E. Gaebelein, *Christian Education in a Democracy*, p. 185.

82. G. Emmett Carter, *The Modern Challenge to Religious Education: God's Message and Our Response* (New York: Sadlier, 1961), pp. 333-337.

83. Harold Carlton Mason, *Abiding Values in Christian Education*, pp. 131-141.

84. Josef Andreas Jungmann, *Handing on the Faith*, pp. 70-71.

85. Johannes Hofinger, "The Catechetical Apostolate of Lay Teachers," in *Lumen Vitae*, XII (October-December, 1957), especially p. 652. Hofinger makes a similar point in *The Art of Teaching Christian Doctrine*, pp. 205-206.

86. Lois E. LeBar, *Focus on People in Church Education* (Westwood, New Jersey: Revell, 1968), pp. 23-24. Also on this matter, see Johannes Hofinger with William Reedy, *The ABC's of Modern Catechetics* (New York: Sadlier, 1962), p. 29.

87. Josef Andreas Jungmann, *Handing on the Faith*, p. 75. On the personality of the teacher, see Clarence H. Benson, *The Christian Teacher*, pp. 49-57; and Lois E. LeBar, *Children in the Bible School*, pp. 35-37.

88. Frank E. Gaebelein, *Christian Education in a Democracy*, p. 187.

89. Johannes Hofinger, *The Art of Teaching Christian Doctrine*, p. 197.

90. This particular phraseology is Jungmann's. Josef Andreas Jungmann, *Handing on the Faith*, p. 71. Also see Frank E. Gaebelein, *Christian Education in a Democracy*, p. 186; and G. Emmett Carter, *The Modern Challenge to Religious Education*, pp. 342-343.

91. Johannes Hofinger, *The Art of Teaching Christian Doctrine*, p. 200; Lois E. LeBar, *Children in the Bible School*, pp. 33-34; and G. Emmett Carter, *The Modern Challenge to Religious Education*, p. 343.

92. *Ibid.*, p. 342.

93. Johannes Hofinger, *The Art of Teaching Christian Doctrine*, p. 201.

94. Frank E. Gaebelein, *Christian Education in a Democracy*, p. 186.

95. D. K. Reisinger, "Teacher Training," in *An Introduction to Evangelical Christian Education*, p. 98.

96. Clarence H. Benson, *The Sunday School in Action*, p. 122.

97. Clarence H. Benson, *The Christian Teacher*, p. 209.

98. See, for example, D. K. Reisinger, "Teacher Training," in *An Introduction to Evangelical Christian Education*, pp. 96-106, and C. B. Eavey, *Principles of Teaching for Christian Teachers*, pp. 96-123. Clarence H. Benson has also written extensively on the Evangelical viewpoint concerning the matter of training teachers for Sunday schools.

99. The term "religious" commonly denotes a person who has taken religious vows, for example, a nun.

100. Josef Andreas Jungmann, *Handing on the Faith*, p. 72.

101. *Ibid.*, pp. 70-76, and Johannes Hofinger, *The Art of Teaching Christian Doctrine*, pp. 197-260. Also see Frank B. Norris, "The Catechetics Course in the Major Seminary"; Mary Carol Francis, "Catechetical Formation of Religious"; and Raymond Lucker and Theodore Stone, "Formation and Training of Lay Catechists," in Johannes Hofinger and Theodore Stone, editors, *Pastoral Catechetics* (New York: Herder and Herder, 1964), pp. 213-225, 226-238, and 239-262.

102. Josef Andreas Jungmann, *Handing on the Faith*, pp. 174-217.

103. Johannes Hofinger, *The Art of Teaching Christian Doctrine*, pp. 62-73.

104. *Ibid.*, p. 25.

105. Marcel van Caster, "The Spirit of the Religion Course," *Lumen Vitae*, VI (July-September, 1951), p. 438.

106. Frank E. Gaebelein, *Christian Education in a Democracy*, p. 198.

107. Lois E. LeBar, *Education That Is Christian*, p. 20.

108. Harold Carlton Mason, *Abiding Values in Christian Education*, p. 98.

109. Lois E. LeBar, *Education That Is Christian*, p. 230; see also pp. 49-118 and 203-245.

110. Lois E. LeBar, *Focus on People in Church Education*, pp. 23-24.

111. Donald M. Joy, *Meaningful Learning in the Church* (Winona Lake, Indiana: Light and Life, 1969), p. 10.

112. Josef Andreas Jungmann, *Handing on the Faith*, p. 79.

113. For example, Frank E. Gaebelein, *Christian Education in a Democracy*, p. 227.

114. Josef Andreas Jungmann, *Handing on the Faith*, p. 79.

115. Frank E. Gaebelein, *Christian Education in a Democracy*, p. 259.

116. Lois E. LeBar, *Education That Is Christian*, p. 135.

117. *Ibid.*, p. 136.

118. Frank E. Gaebelein, *Christian Education in a Democracy*, p. 270.

119. Lois E. LeBar, *Education That Is Christian*, p. 26.

120. Josef Andreas Jungmann, *Handing on the Faith*, p. 125.

121. "Christian schools" refers to either Protestant or Catholic schools, especially day or boarding schools.

122. Frank E. Gaebelein, *Christian Education in a Democracy*, pp. 269-270.

123. Josef Andreas Jungmann, *Handing on the Faith*, p. 77.

124. Frank E. Gaebelein, "Toward a Philosophy of Christian Education," in *An Introduction to Evangelical Christian Education*, p. 45.

125. Johannes Hofinger, *The Art of Teaching Christian Doctrine*, especially pp. 199-202.

Chapter III

The Social-Cultural Theoretical Approach to Religious Education

CRITERIA FOR THE SOCIAL-CULTURAL APPROACH

The social-cultural approach to theorizing about religious education is delineated by the following criteria. *First,* theological conceptualizations are open to continual change in such a way that experience, interpreted by scientific methodology, is normative for religion itself as well as for religious education theory and practice. The Bible is considered to be a religious educational resource. *Second,* religious education is essentially concerned with social and cultural reconstruction rather than with an individualized salvation. *Third,* the religion teacher's task is to create social consciousness and to develop social living skills by arranging situations in which students participate directly in the social process. *Fourth,* the Christian personality and Christian life-style of the student arise from the development of his latent personal and religious capacities.[1]

It might also be noted that neither the dimension of the supernatural nor the concept of the church plays a major role in the theorizing of typical social-culturally oriented religious educationists. Teaching practices developed from within the social-cultural approach often feature the group (students and teacher) living life together in the world.

ANTECEDENTS TO THE SOCIAL-CULTURAL APPROACH

Theological reorientation

The social-cultural theoretical approach to religious education is a radical departure from the historic, theologically and biblically founded religious educational endeavor of the

59

church. Social-cultural theorists look upon the historic religious educational endeavor as lamentably defective because of its rigid adherence to the "iron-clad theory" that religious education is primarily concerned with the communication of a divinely ordained message.

The focus of the social-cultural approach is upon the individual and the society of which he is a member, rather than upon the content of a supernatural message. The "swing of things," for social-cultural theorists, is not metaphysical but scientific; they seek "not the formal but the real."[2] This theological reorientation of religious educational theory was fueled, in part, by the impact of nineteenth century European scholars, such as Ferdinand Christian Bauer, who advocated an essentially humanistic approach to the understanding of the Bible; Albrect Ritschl, who insisted that Christianity was at root practical rather than theological; and Charles Darwin, whose writings connected human life directly to this world. Instead of beginning with the historic beliefs of the churches, social-cultural theorists believe that religious educational theory and practice "should be based upon the best scientific knowledge available in regard to the nature of man and the conditions for his growth."[3] Wayne Rood has called this transferring of faith from a metaphysical to a scientific object "the outstanding theological phenomenon of the twentieth century."[4]

Educational reorientation

George Coe once remarked that: "It goes without saying that both the processes and the aims of religious education intertwine with those of so-called secular education. The relation is more than intertwining; they are branches of the same tree, they partake of the same sap."[5] The antecedents to the theoretical and practical viewpoints which came to be characteristic both of secular education and of the social-cultural approach to religious education include the theoretical notions of Johann Pestalozzi (1746-1827), Friedrich Froebel (1782-1852), Horace Bushnell (1802-1876), and John Dewey (1859-1952).

Pestalozzi's educational theories were rooted in the psychological movement that flowered in the nineteenth century. He believed that the individual person was essentially good in much the same way that Rousseau suggested in the famous opening passage in *Emile*: "Out of God's hands come good things, it is by man's hands that these good things become evil."[6] Pestalozzi's argument to the effect that love for God results from loving one's fellow men was of particular importance to the development of that religious educational theory which came to typify the social-cultural approach. Effective educational practice, according to this Swiss educational innovator, must follow the order of nature. He insisted that the verbalism characteristic of so much education should be replaced with an educational process based on relevant relationships capable of being fully comprehended by the child.[7]

Froebel, who was much influenced by Pestalozzi, also found man's nature to be basically good. He asserted that the divine essence of man might be unfolded and lifted into consciousness through education. Thus, man would be able to consciously and freely obey the divine principle that was within him. Accordingly, for Froebel, religious education was less redemptive in character than it was a kind of awakening, or reawakening, of the already present religious element. As to educational practice, this "children's champion" valued the educative power of play, and he advocated teaching methods that made extensive use of self-activity.[8]

Horace Bushnell seems, albeit inadvertently, to have addressed himself directly to the issues that eventually shaped the religious education movement in America. In this way he probably made his greatest contribution to the twentieth century. *Christian Nurture* (1861),[9] Bushnell's best known book (the first edition of which was published in 1847 as *Views of Christian Nurture and Subjects Adjacent Thereto*), is a religious and educational classic. In answer to his own question, "What is the true idea of Christian education?" Bushnell answered, "That the child is to grow up a Christian, and never know himself as being otherwise."[10] A. J. Wm. Myers says that Bushnell's widely quoted answer has been one of the most dynamic sentences in religious education. The ideal embodied is the aim of all progressive education."[11] Bushnell is best remembered by religious educationists for having sought another than the traditional revival technique for bringing children into a knowledge of and relationship with God. His approach, reminiscent of Froebel, was that religious education ought to nurture the religious bud that was already present in the child. This New England pastor fought the transmissive approach by suggesting that children do not receive religion as goods received into a warehouse. His proposal for a religious education based on the concepts of growth and nurture amounted to training children *in the way that they are expected to live.*[12]

Some other religious educational tenets for which Bushnell is remembered are that (1) the home is the proper center of religious training, (2) growth, not conquest, is the true means of extending God's kingdom, (3) teaching should suit the age of the pupil, and (4) experience rather than doctrine is the best foundation for teaching religion.[13] Bushnell's importance to religious education does not seem to be so much that he formulated educational theory as *that he thought the thoughts that were foundational* for the theoretical and practical perspective which eventually became characteristic of the social-cultural theoretical approach to religious education. In addition, his thought (especially his theological opinion) is also seminal for the contemporary theological approach to religious education to be described in a succeeding chapter.

John Dewey's philosophical doctrines and progressive educational proposals may be counted among the most significant of the factors which have given form to the social-cultural theoretical approach to religious education. His philosophical redefinition of knowledge and learning, though totally antithetical to the traditional theoretical concepts of religious education discussed in the preceding chapter, became a theoretical fundament of the social-cultural position. The historical, traditional viewpoint on religious education held that knowledge (and most especially religious knowledge) was an assemblage of absolute truths and certainties *grasped by the mind*; that learning came about through the communication (transmission) of these truths and certainties; and that religious (i.e. moral) behavior followed right learning as a matter of course. Dewey, on the other hand, taught that knowledge might best be thought of as modified action resulting from experience; that mind should be described as a tool by which experience may be sharpened and made more meaningful; that learning may not be distinguished from the living of life's experiences (episodes) which beget knowledge (i.e. modify action); and that moral acts, which are wholly social, come before the thought.[14]

The progressive education movement in education (commonly identified with John Dewey, but which should not be confused with his philosophical thought)[15] was really an attitude toward educational practice which was in revolt against traditional formal education. The following characteristics of the progressive education movement seem to have had a strong influence upon the development of the social-cultural theoretical approach to religious education: *first*, its willingness to give a considerable amount of self-directed freedom to individual students; *second*, its emphasis upon interest rather than punishment as the source of discipline; *third*; its encouragement of overt purposeful activity; *fourth*, its focus upon growth factors in the child; *fifth*, its application of scientifically derived pedagogical principles in the classroom; *sixth*, its tailoring of instruction to different kinds and classes of children; and *seventh*, its tendency to move beyond the school program into the community—an attitude related to the conviction that education is a part of life and not just a preparation for it.[16]

Dewey's theoretical and practical notions significantly affected the development of the social-cultural theoretical approach to religious education through the integration of his philosophical, moral, and educational ideas into the professional training programs and literature of the so-called religious educational movement, especially during the earlier decades of the twentieth century.[17]

The Religious Education Association

The founding of the Religious Education Association in 1903 may be taken as an event which represented a crystalizing of the forces which culminated in the formation of the social-cultural approach to theorizing about religious education. William Rainey Harper, at one time the president of the University of Chicago, was instrumental in the sponsoring and founding of this Association which grew out of a 1903 meeting of leading American educators in Chicago. John Dewey, who gave a major address[18] at the meeting, was the leader and principal spokesman for a number of those present who hoped that the proposed association would become mainly an agency for enriching secular education. Another point of view, enunciated by George Coe in a celebrated address bearing upon the theme of salvation by education,[19] was that the new association should have religious education as a primary interest. Coe's position won out, and the association became The Religious Education Association. The original stated aims of the Association were: "To inspire the religious forces of our country with the educational ideal; to inspire the educational forces of our country with the religious ideal; and to keep before the public mind the ideal of moral and religious education and the sense of its need and value."[20]

Although John Dewey drifted out of the Religious Education Association, his views continued to have a formative influence upon the theoretical and practical positions adopted by its leaders. It should also be noted that even though this Association never took an official stance toward either the theory or the practice of religious education, a careful reading of *Religious Education,* its official journal, indicates that a preponderance of the articles appearing on its pages during the first thirty-five years of its existence (1906-1940) were written from an essentially social-cultural perspective.

REPRESENTATIVE SOCIAL-CULTURAL THEORISTS

George Coe is by almost any standard of reference the most influential of the educationists whose books have been selected as representative of the social-cultural approach to religious education. Coe, whose major book is generally acknowledged to be *A Social Theory of Religious Education* (1917),[21] may well have been the most widely read and followed Protestant religious educational thinker during the first half of the twentieth century. His theoretical position is fully within the parameters of the social-cultural approach; *A Social Theory,* indeed, is an extended exposition of and application of the principles underlying this school of thought. When he determined to think through the problems of religious education anew under the presuppositions of modern science, Coe accepted the possibility that traditional theologically derived aims and teaching practices would be found useless. He proposed, eventually, that the traditional aim of individual salvation would have to be replaced by the broader aim of social reconstruction, and that transmissively intentioned teaching practices would have to be abandoned for vital participation in social interaction. Coe's perception of religious education, then, is antithetical to the traditional theological position that the teacher as an instrument of the church transmits Christianity to the student. He contends that the teacher and student should involve themselves together in the venture of re-creating Christianity itself. Hence, his widely quoted (and misquoted) statement: "Religion changes in the act of teaching it."[22] Within a re-created Christianity (conceptualized by Coe as a democracy of God) the loyalty of the Christian would not be to one person (even to Jesus); rather, his loyalty would be to society, *to persons.*[23]

William Clayton Bower is probably the second most influential representative social-cultural theorist. His book, *The Curriculum of Religious Education* (1925),[24] was a standard of the religious education movement during the second quarter of the twentieth century. Bower, a prolific writer, addresses his books to a number of reading publics including public school teachers and administrators as well as religious educators. One of his major concerns is the introduction of scientific methodology to all levels of the religious educational endeavor. This concern is especially noticeable in his books dealing with church school matters, for example, *A Survey of Religious Education in the Local Church* (1919).[25] Bower's greatest attention focuses upon the problem of how personality development might best be guided along desirable lines. He concludes that personality develops continuously as a result of experience. Bower conceptualizes experience as being the interaction between the person and his environment. By controlling experience, he theorizes, the direction of personality growth may be predicted and controlled. *The Curriculum of Religious Education* applies Bower's theories concerning personality development toward a proposed program for religious education. *Moral and Spiritual Values in Education* (1952)[26] extends these theories into a plan for value education in public school settings.

The third major representative social-cultural theorist is Ernest Chave. His book, *A Functional Approach to Religious Education* (1947)[27] carries the basic principles of the social-cultural school of thought somewhat further along naturalistic lines than either Coe or Bower propose. (In this connection, James Smart believes that Chave merely accepts the implications of this social-cultural way of thinking and that he then follows it through to its logical conclusion.)[28] Chave totally rejects the historic formulation of the Christian faith; he contends that the two greatest hindrances to religious education are *sectarianism* which he believes to be a divisive loyalty to one religion and *supernaturalism* which he claims is founded upon a prescientific world view and, at best, results in a blurred faith in a supposedly personal God. He argues that religious education cannot look to traditional theological sources for its message, methods, or incentives; "it must find them in the growing present." The basic assumption upon which Chave proceeds to develop his version of the social-cultural approach to religious education is that religion itself arises, here and now, from the primary adjustments of life. Chave appears to be a consistent social-culturist in his understanding of the social aims of religious education, of the teacher as an arranger of this process, and of the student as having all the needed spiritual potential within himself by which he may rise through social interaction to a fully functional level of religious living.[29]

Coe, Bower, and Chave have been selected as the principal representative theorists of the social-cultural approach. However, the books of two other theorists, Sophia Lyon Fahs and George Herbert Betts, are written from a similar perspective and have proven helpful to this investigation. In her books, especially *Today's Children and Yesterday's Heritage* (1952),[30] Fahs has given practical expression to many of the theoretical notions typical of the social-cultural approach. Bett's viewpoints, probably best stated in *How to Teach Religion* (1919),[31] are in basic, but not always full, agreement with the social-cultural approach.

ANALYSIS OF THE SOCIAL-CULTURAL APPROACH

The Aim

Genesis of aim

Social ideals exert a determining influence on the aim of religious education for social-cultural theorists. For true-to-type theorists of this school of thought, aim is a working construct radicated in present social issues. Traditional theological conceptualizations are looked upon as being incapable of generating aims that are sufficiently comprehensive to encompass the complexities of modern life. Social-cultural theorists believe that religious education must develop aims which (1) demonstrate faith in a developmental process, (2) meaningfully account for human experience, and (3) creatively point the way to the solution of current social issues through the coordination of latent spiritual forces that would otherwise lie dormant within society. The theological rationale for this viewpoint is stated most clearly by George Coe in his celebrated article, "The Idea of God": ". . . the modern mind has also learned to think of God as most intimately related to the process of the world. Much of the older Christian thought represented God and the world as two separate realities, as though the world of nature were distinct from another world called the supernatural. But any such distinction as this between the natural and the divine is no longer tenable."[32] Attention to present social issues, then, is perceived by social-cultural thinkers as being equivalent to listening to the "call of God."

Creative aspect of aim

Social-cultural theorists, rejecting those aims of religious education which are stated in terms of handing on a divinely ordained message, have proposed that religious educational processes should enter creatively "into the flow of present existence." Religious education, accordingly, ceases to be a means by which revealed doctrines and ancient standards are transmitted; it becomes instead a process whereby these doctrines and standards are themselves revised. Thus, Ernest Chave states that: "Religious education must cease to be the tool of conservatism, indoctrinating immature minds with outgrown ideas and futile customs. It must stimulate creative thought, reconstructing concepts of God, redefining spiritual objectives, and reorganizing religious programs."[33] In a similar vein Sophia Lyon Fahs declares that: "No longer can religious education be the simple process of instructing children in a way already decided upon as the best; no longer can it be a passing on of moral principles. . . . Religious growth and education in religion we must learn to conceive of as a process of questioning, of experimenting, in thought and in conduct."[34]

The concept of continuous creation has been seized upon by social-cultural theorists in support of this creative approach to the understanding of religious educational aim. These theorists believe that traditional theological aims have usually resulted in the notion that the growth of God's kingdom is merely the quantitative increase of something that is already qualitatively finished. Continuous creation, on the other hand, affords a rationale for aims targeted toward growth in a qualitative sense, a "coming into being of something unprecedented and unpredictable . . . involving possibly the superseding of some ancient good."[35] According to social-cultural theorists, such creative aims will lead to the adoption of Christ's creative spirit and thus enable Christians (who have accepted the burdens and risks of re-creating the Christian faith itself) to maintain vital continuity with Christ by following him upon his road of discovery and creation.[36]

This creative approach to the aims of religious education, according to typical social-cultural thinking, could become the supreme corrective for the spiritual malaise which seemingly afflicts modern youth, by enabling them to participate with God and their fellow men in the creation of a "really new" order of society. This new social order would be targeted toward universally good social experience, and it would deal creatively with the deepest personal and social values. The social-cultural school of thought maintains that a continual *becoming* is both the end and the process by which both personal and social ideals, at their highest levels, may be achieved and maintained. "According to this point of view," affirms William Clayton Bower, "education is vastly more and other than something that can be determined by adults and imposed from without upon passive and receptive learners, however skillful the techniques of inculcation may be. It is nothing less than *the initiation of the young into a creative personal and social experience.*"[37]

Scope of aim

The scope of aim for religious educationists of the social-cultural school of thought is largely encompassed by the notion of a "kingdom of God" (or, as in Coe's later writings, a "democracy of God"), an idealized social order in which the principles enunciated most clearly by Jesus Christ will be actualized. Social-cultural theorists find the individualized salvific goals and the supernaturalistic interpretation of the kingdom of God characteristic of traditional theorizing too pessimistic to be acceptable. George Coe, for example, states that: ". . . our generation has come to see that the redemptive mission of the Christ is nothing less than that of transforming the social order itself into a brotherhood or family of God. We are not saved, each by himself, and then added to one another like marbles in a bag. . . . "[38] Similarly, Sophia Lyon Fahs maintains that: "If our long-time goal is the salvation of a world community rather than merely the salvation of a few select individuals . . . our concept of individual responsibility is changed. . . . We no longer feel like racers each rushing to gain his own crown of glory. . . . We feel as learners, adventurers, experimenters. With God living in us, we seek together to find out how to bring new values into living, how to widen our feelings of fellowship—not with saints alone but with all kinds of people."[39]

The "democracy of God" envisioned by Coe and other social-culturally oriented religious educationists is a unification that goes beyond "the hooking together of ecclesiastical machines"; it is to be accomplished only through the coming together of persons in the unsectarian spirit characteristic of the sciences. Union on the basis of "faith and order," from this viewpoint, amounts to little more than "a pooling of inefficiencies." The achievement of a synthesis of modern life through the rediscovery of moral and spiritual values is. perceived by these theorists as a problem for the whole democratic community, not just a matter for the churches. The kind of religious experience (and "habit of mind") that must of necessity underlie a dynamic coming together which might eventuate in an operative "democracy of God" must, according to this school of thought, be based upon a reborn religious education which has an adequately broad scope of aim.[40]

Social and moral dimensions of aim

The democratic ideal, a conviction that individual destinies and the destiny of society are interdependent, is a notion which social-cultural theorists seem to have inherited from John Dewey. In the sense that the term is commonly used by these theorists, democracy has to do with the self-realizing of persons as they live out their lives in a shared social situation. This philosophy places a fundamental emphasis upon persons as persons and upon human values as superseding all other values. From this viewpoint, moral character is not related to religious practices such as Bible reading or attendance of worship; it is perceived to be totally a matter of man's relationship to society, a relationship that may best be promoted by a creatively conceived education rooted in the concrete social situation. Four fundamental considerations seem to underlie the typical view of religious education which flows from the democratic ideal: *first,* that learning is a social process, knowledge, itself, being primarily a social creation; *second,* that the Christian religion (indeed, all religion) is fundamentally social; *third,* that in religious education "immature persons are being prepared to take their places in a specialized Christian institution, a social community of like-minded persons, known as the church"; and *fourth,* that the social responsibilities of the Christian religion are by nature functional.[41]

The most famous social-culturally oriented statement of religious educational aim is that put forward by George Coe in *A Social Theory of Religious Education:* "Granted this social idealism as the interpretation of the life that now is, the aim of Christian education becomes this: *Growth of the young toward and into mature and efficient devotion to the democracy of God, and happy self-realization therein.*"[42]

In explanation of the above statement which is based precisely upon his commitment to the democratic ideal, Coe gives negative criticism of the assumptions that typically underlie traditional theological formulations of aim: *first,* aims which propose instruction in things which a Christian ought to know assume that religion consists essentially of a completed, authoritative revelation which must be handed on from generation to generation; *second,* aims which point to preparation for membership in the church assume that the church is the authoritative administrator of the fixed revelation; and *third,* conceptions of aim which purport to save the child's soul are based on a doctrine of redemption which calls upon the person to live separately from the world, rather than to work out his salvation within the world.[43] By way of contrast, the foundation considerations for the social-cultural aim of *"Growth of the young toward and into mature and efficient devotion to the democracy of God, and happy self-realization therein"* are, according to Coe: *first,* that no separation exists between the divine society and the human society because the social instincts provide the rudimentary conditions for such a divine-human democracy; *second,* that devotion to a social cause is not the equivalent of crossing a line which separates the saved from the unsaved ("The lover accepts no security that does not include his loved ones"); *third,* that efficiency suggests the necessity for concrete evidence of achievement which can be measured; and *fourth,* that there must be a lessening of individualism through growing participation in the creation of an ideal society by which the pupil will gain life and realize fellowship with the Father.[44]

The specific social issues, constituting the call of God, to which Coe believes the aim of religious education must address itself are: (1) *social welfare,* which has to do with the nonhuman environment, i.e. disease, etc.; (2) *social justice,* which touches the parts that men play in each other's lives; and (3) *a world society,* which involves the integration of all mankind into a single, democratically governed brotherhood.[45]

The immediate aims of an adequately socialized education which would tend to promote the realization of the ultimate religious educational ends as advanced by Coe are: that the student shall (1) acquire the tools of social intercourse—language, number, social forms, etc.; (2) be introduced to society through the sciences, arts, literature, and most especially through participation in social life; (3) be trained for an occupation; and (4) be intelligently socialized by the shaping of the motives of his conduct.[46]

William Clayton Bower and Ernest Chave have also worked out apparently consistent social-cultural statements of aim (function) for religious education. The objectives of modern religious education as formulated by Bower are: *first,* to help growing persons, through the orientation of the whole self, to achieve a Christlike personality; *second,* to bring society under the ideals of Christ in the progressive realization of the kingdom of God; *third,* to make the resources of the Christian faith available for dealing with the issues of the day; and *fourth,* to build a sustaining fellowship—which is the church and which will be supportive of commitment to God's causes.[47] Chave proposed that a new day for religious education might be achieved by incorporating an analysis of the functions of religion directly into the aims of religious educational programs. His own research resulted in the development of ten functional categories intended to be descriptive of the way religion operates in growing lives. Chave's ten categories, considerably abreviated, are: (1) a sense of personal worth in recognition of one's being as a creative member of the universe; (2) social sensitivity—awareness of other person's potentialities; (3) appreciation of the universe; (4) ability to discriminate among values; (5) responsibility and accountability—one cannot be a law unto one's self; (6) cooperative fellowship—ability to contribute to a transformed group life; (7) quest for truth and realization of values—religion is a persistent quest, an effort to extend spiritual learnings and to realize human possibilities; (8) integration of life's experiences into a working philosophy of life; (9) appreciation of historical continuity—reflection upon experiences both of one's own life and of the lives of others in search of cosmic meanings and universal principles of conduct; and (10) participation in group celebrations in order to keep goals and beliefs in the focus of attention.[48] The assumption which Chave makes is that: ". . . wherever and whenever these kinds of experiences are being developed spiritual goals are being realized, whether they take place in church, home, school, playground, business, or other relationship."[49]

George Herbert Betts bases his approach to the aims of religious education upon the fundamental assumption that "Children can be brought to a religious character and experience through right nurture and training in religion."[50] The end which religious education seeks, according to Betts, is certain desired changes in the life, thought, and experience of the student. This aim may be tested by whether the student does, in fact, live differently in the here and now as a result of his religious education. Betts contends, that since life itself sets the aim, a proper question to ask is, "What are the demands that life makes on the individual? . . . What abilities must he have trained in order that he may most completely express God's plan for his life?"[51] Betts concludes that the aim of teaching religion may be summarized by three great requirements that life places upon every individual: *first,* fruitful knowledge of religious truths that can be used in daily life; *second,* right attitudes of warmth and loyalty that will eventuate in worthwhile actions; and *third,* skill in living and in the conduct of daily life.[52]

The Content

Content is not something to be handed on

Social-culturally oriented religious educationists are unanimous in their rejection of the traditional theological notion that the content of religious education is essentially a divinely authoritative message—be it "saving truth" or "way of life"—that must be transmitted unchanged from generation to generation. These theorists usually agree that traditional transmissive conceptualizations of religious education are to some extent logical. And they admit that a "propagandistic approach" makes the identification of content and the selection of materials a less difficult process than a typical social-cultural approach is likely to make it (because children can be given subject matter thought to have been most successful in bringing about acceptance, conversion, and loyalty to a particular position).[53] Nonetheless, George Coe charges, such content-oriented, transmissively intentioned religious education not only does not work; "it also, of its own nature, creates evils for which it is loathe to accept responsibility."[54] Among the evils of content-oriented education cited by Coe are (1) that it employs force, including psychic force, to outwardly achieve its aims, (2) that it brings some men into subjection to other men, even though its intentions are to promote obedience to God, and (3) that its achievements sometimes run counter to its own objectives because it does not, by rigorous analysis, keep abreast of changing conditions.[55]

Another line of thinking followed by some social-cultural theorists is that content-oriented teaching places in the mind nonfunctional facts. Such facts play no part in shaping life's ideals; they merely lie like so much rubbish in the mind, dulling the edge of learning interest and making the achievement of desired goals less likely.[56] For this reason, Ernest Chave contends that religious education "cannot look backward for its message, methods, or incentives but must find them in the growing present."[57] A similar sentiment is enunciated by George Coe: ". . . if we would press toward a democracy of God, we must turn the attention of pupils to many matters that are this side of the biblical horizon."[58]

Content is present living

The content of religious education, from the social-cultural viewpoint, encompasses all of life's possible experiences as they are enriched, interpreted, and controlled in terms of purposes in harmony with the Christian ideal. From this perspective, content is indistinguishable from teaching method. Thus, religious education becomes actual guided experience in living the Christian life. The qualities of religious thinking and of responsible living are best nurtured through deliberately planned student participation in life experiences as a "real part" of the world's working force. Social interaction, then, is regarded as the "basal process" of religious education and of social reconstruction. Hence, religious education and social reconstruction should take place together.[59]

George Coe elaborates upon the here-and-now focus of religious educational *content* which is to be found in present relations and interactions between persons. Coe holds that religious educational practices (rooted in the incarnational notion that God makes himself known to man in concrete human life) should consist fundamentally of arranging conditions in which love is experienced, exercised, and deliberately lived. He theorizes that the intellectual and faith capacities fostered by these practices will sustain a lifelong Christian pattern of living. More practically, Coe suggests that a socially grounded religious education might well include the involvement of students with persons who really love *both them and others.* Involvement with loving persons should be followed by the deliberate expansion of the student's social attachments, for example, by merging family loyalties into humane interests of wider scope. This kind of *practice in loving,* Coe insists, provides a basis for a truly vital theory of religious instruction in which there is no longer the deadly separation of knowing from doing, of Christian doctrine from Christian experience. By thus radicating religious educational content in present social interaction, he believes, it is possible to fuse love and faith, "so that even in childhood the voice of God and the voice of human need shall be one voice."[60]

Subject-matter content

For social-cultural theorists, then, content of religious education is social experience, not printed facts which can be mastered. "The Word made flesh," not in an historical event but in those human relations that accompany teaching, is looked upon as by far the most effective factor in religious education. Nonetheless, subject-matter content is a topic of considerable interest to social-culturally oriented religious educationists.

One initial assumption of this viewpoint seems to be that there is no specifically religious subject matter (or religious knowledge) because spiritual and material reality are perceived to have an interdependent natural relationship. These theorists assert that subject matter can and should be drawn from "anything, anywhere"—from scripture, history, church life, the world of present experience, "the early lilacs," and "the sow's pink litter." However, it is strongly maintained that the principle of social interaction must be determinative of that subject matter which is allowed to be inserted into the religious educational program—because the traditional separation between living and preparing to live must not be allowed to reenter the religious educational process via subject-matter content. In addition, subject matter that is not specifically social (for example, physical science) is to be treated as social in the sense that it is of common interest to society—and to God.[61]

William Clayton Bower remarks that, if the content of religious education is understood in the manner described above, the specific content of the religious education curriculum is constituted of these elements: (1) the situation as it is being lived; (2) the past experience which the learner brings to the learning situation and which is his first resource in interpreting and dealing with new experiences; and (3) the experience of the race itself as it is communicated (in many ways) to individual students—thus making it unnecessary to begin totally anew each time a situation is faced.[62] (One prime example of racial experience, according to Bower, is the Bible.)[63]

In the selection of subject matter, George Herbert Betts maintains that two principles are to be observed: (1) it is to be suited to the aims that are sought; and (2) it is to be adapted to the student. The "great law" to be observed in the ordering subject matter is that it must be arranged psychologically.[64] Although his approach to subject matter focuses upon the child and his capacities rather than upon a revealed message, it seems to bring about a separation of religious education content from the living of life that is not in full accord with the social-cultural approach.

The Bible, the major source of content for traditional theologically oriented religious educationists is, at best, merely a religious educational resource for social-cultural theorists. Traditional theorists go to the Bible to find out God's thoughts and feelings about men. Social-cultural theorists, for their part, typically believe the Bible to be only a collection of records concerning human experiences.[65] George Coe, for example, holds that the Bible is a uniquely powerful body of social literature which will not be supplanted as a significant religious educational resource even though in and of itself it cannot communicate divine life to man. Accordingly, he assigns the Bible its place as one of many means for promoting and awakening that divine life among men that is theoretically communicated only by living itself (i.e. social process).[66]

The Teacher

To the question, "Shall religion teaching be conceptualized in terms of handing on a religion or shall it be conceptualized in terms of participation with students in the creation of a new world?" social-cultural theorists have generally responded that the latter is the only "real" possibility. Underlying the rationale for this conception of religious education is the conviction that living the Christian life does not differ from expertness in any other practical activity. This is especially true because religious education is not considered to be qualitatively advanced by the reception of a supposedly divinely ordained message. The aim of teaching, then, is not to risk invasion of the students' personalities by imposing truth upon them; rather, it is to promote individual personal growth through skillfully guided participation in a group, thus emancipating each and every student into full and active membership in the "democracy of God."[67]

Social-cultural theorists typically argue that transmissive modes of teaching children are likely to produce adults who "settle historical and scientific questions without historical or scientific study, and by the results [judge whether their] neighbors are sheep or goats."[68] On the other hand, these theorists contend, teaching which consists mainly in guiding growing students into meaningful group experience will, more probably, educate these students for an adulthood characterized by high ideals and effective social skills.[69]

The teacher's qualifications

From the social-cultural viewpoint, religion teachers are qualified by competence in certain necessary skills—which may be taught to intelligent and willing persons. Such standards for qualifications, based not upon personal considerations but upon demonstrable skills, would relieve (at least in theory) many of the strains which exist in church school endeavors because teachers could be assigned, transferred, promoted, or discharged on impersonal educational grounds. In the ideal democracy of God every worker could be counted upon to acquiesce in all decisions, even those running against personal desires, providing these decisions were supported by evidence that a more efficient religious education would ensue.

Personality is another qualification for teaching religion often mentioned by social-culturally oriented writers. Nothing, it is maintained, will take the place of a wholesome and winning personality that actually experiences and, in turn, admits others into the experience and fellowship of the Christian life. However, typical social-cultural theorists do not consider personality to be a gift from the gods. They hold that the teacher's personality is caused as "everything is caused." Hence, the ideal teacher's winning personality is made, not born. In essence, personality can therefore be counted among the skills which a teacher can be held responsible to learn and to exhibit.[70]

The teacher's training

Social interaction is at the core of social-culturally conceived teacher training. A potential teacher is not taught a "bag of tricks" which will make him think that he can teach religion at some future time; he is immediately immersed in the social process that is religious education. For this reason, George Coe has advanced these principles for a program to train teachers in the local parish: *first,* that training in the motive to teach is the cornerstone of the whole enterprise—it consists of enlisting the parental instinct as an active core around which society may be transformed into the family of God; *second,* that the material for such a program is primarily one's interaction with particular children, and only secondarily books; and *third,* that training the teacher does not occur in isolation from the actual work of the school, but ideas (which are essential to the development of skills) must be inserted into the program—"skill is achieved by the fusion of doing and thinking."[71]

The difficulties encountered in effectively training teachers in the time usually available in parish situations have brought some social-cultural theorists to the conclusion that the most effective means of improving teaching is through supervised practice.[72] Supervision, as understood by these theorists, is dynamically rooted in the social-interactional process. It offers a practical way which is consistent with their theoretical view-point for many unhappy conditions to be changed, and it affords one way of putting a professional element into certain otherwise chaotic situations. The supervisor, though, is not a "super," but a recognized co-worker who is appointed because of a felt need and a desired outcome.[73] George Coe, for example, takes for granted that the fundamental idea in supervision is intimate sharing of those burdens and blames that sometimes fall heavily upon isolated individuals.[74]

The teacher's method

From the social-cultural theoretical perspective, the content and the method of religious education are inseparable realities. It has been suggested, if a distinction must be made, that content might be thought of as the material (the "stuff") of experience while method is the way of dealing with it. Thus, content and method are looked upon as being determinative of each other. One consequence of this way of conceptualizing religious education content and method is that religious beliefs, attitudes, and overt behaviors are considered to be influenced more by the shape of the experience itself than by the biblical or doctrinal subject matter that may be inserted into experience. If this is true, Ernest Chave maintains, the end point of religious education must be considered in the selection of methods employed by the teacher. When, for example, creative responses are desired, methods of transmissive indoctrination which are likely to be productive of conformity must be rejected in favor of democratic procedures which tend to lead to creative kinds of behavior.[75] The social-culturally oriented teacher, then, uses social interaction as his overall method, but he is responsible for making deliberate use of such other individual methods as may have shown themselves to be productive of the goals he has selected. Theoretically, one major characteristic of teaching practices based upon these social-culturally oriented principles is that the teacher functions democratically as a guide to "forthreaching" rather than to "passive" students. It should be noted that the center of social-cultural attention to method is the student's learning rather than the teacher's teaching.[76]

The scientific development of dependable teaching methods by means of regulated observation and experiment has been proposed by several social-cultural theorists, notably George Coe and William Clayton Bower.[77] Coe maintains that the discovery of "laws" relating to the "measured relations of antecedence and consequence" would make it possible to reintroduce the notion of control in religious education, not in a "schoolmasterish" sense, but in the sense that the religion teacher would be in command of a process.[78] Bower is of the opinion that competent application of the factually grounded, experimentally oriented, and predictively intentioned scientific method would not lessen but would positively enhance the religious aspect of the religious education process.[79] This overall process has been analyzed by Bower in terms of several related but not necessarily sequential learning steps: (1) clear realization of the situation; (2) analysis of the issues; (3) past experience of person and of the race; (4) identification of possible outcomes; (5) selection of desired outcomes; (6) experimentation and testing of conclusions; and (7) reduction of desired outcomes, when achieved, to habitual behaviors.[80]

A brief summary of the theory underlying the social-cultural attitude toward teaching method, as well as toward the content of religious education, is stated by Coe: "Social character and efficiency are to be achieved throught social experience; social experience is to be had primarily through the performance of social functions, but it may be extended through imagination in the use of well-selected and well-graded subject matter that represents the social experience of the race; school experience is most effective educationally when the pupil experiences the least break between it and the life of the larger society."[81]

The Student

The student,[82] as understood with the aid of modern science rather than by theological doctrines concerning human nature, is a determining factor in the religious educational scheme proposed by social-cultural theorists. These theorists consider the student, as a product of evolution, to have received both the good and bad fruits of the experience of the race. They reject any theological concept of original sin which severs human relationship with God. The racial heritage is believed to leave the student's religious capacities (which are rooted in his instinctual nature) intact and yet leave him limitless capacities for both good or evil. The laws by which the student may be educated for full participation in the "democracy of God" are within the student himself; they are to be discovered scientifically through controlled observation and experiment, and not through theological speculation. Thus, theoretically, a significant aspect of the religious educational task is to side with creative evolutionary forces in encouraging the higher tendencies. Social-culturally planned religious educational measures are not aimed to press the student into a divinely revealed mold. The purpose of these measures is to free him to creatively work out his relationships with other men, and with God, through active participation in the social process.[83]

The nature of the student

The conception of the student as a living organism, a whole being who develops religiously and socially out of his own resources, is central to the social-cultural theoretical position. William Clayton Bower, for example, attacks the older psychological and theological views which divide the human person into "body" and "soul" or into "natural" and "supernatural" as separate entities, although he agrees that for purposes of description and analysis it may be convenient to think in terms of physicochemical elements, reflexes, impulses, habits, and the like. All of these physical, mental, and spiritual concepts, Bower maintains, are so interdependent that it is not possible to determine their boundaries. The living person, to use his term, is a "functioning whole."[84]

Sophia Lyon Fahs castigates the viewpoint of religious leaders who assume, from a knowledge of theological dogma, that children are "born in sin" and therefore have evil instincts which must be controlled. Fahs contends that students are emotionally dynamic, motivated to struggle toward their own desires, and particularly sensitive to the emotional atmosphere. She holds that even from birth the child is conditioned toward love rather than hostility. If this love turns to hostility, the cause is not a natural propensity toward evil; it is because the child is deprived of love. Fahs appears to base her permissively intentioned teaching methods upon her conviction that human nature is potentially good and that it grows according to a natural schedule.[85] George Coe is of the opinion that children are born "bearing the image of the creator," but that they obviously are candidates for either a good or bad character. The task of religious education is to provide encouragement and support for the better possibilities. (Coe feels that the difficulties for religious education arising from the theological doctrine of depravity are largely overcome in those communions where the countervailing doctrine of baptismal regeneration is accepted.)[86]

The personality of the student

Religious education, as conceived by social-cultural theorists, has a twofold function: (1) to bring about the fullest possible development of whole persons; and (2) to promote social righteousness within a society of growing persons. Students, from this perspective, are the irreducible factor in a religious educational situation. The writings of two social-cultural theorists, namely William Clayton Bower and George Coe, evince an extensive interest in personality, especially its development through education.

Bower considers personality to be primarily a social product, and society, in turn, to be a composition of individual persons whose collective character determines its integrity. He theorizes that the development of personality is influenced by a hierarchy of physical, reflexive, social-interactive, intellective, and valuative factors, For Bower, the last two mentioned factors are of particular salience. Human intelligence, for example, makes possible the creative, conscious, many-sided personal relations (natural, social, and cosmic) which distinguish man from the lower animals. The valuative factor, interacting with the intellective factor, Bower believes, leads to the highest level of human behavior in which intelligent preferential choice makes possible both an organized system of values and a working philosophy of life. The task of religious education, then, "is to help self-realizing persons to discover the potential values as they emerge from their experience in the course of everyday living and to test them by the insights and values of the human past, interpret them, and judge them so as to bring their experience under the discipline of a controlling purpose."[87] Bower concludes from the above line of reasoning that personality is an outgrowth of experience. *Helping growing persons bring their experience under the control of ideas and values* is an even more direct way of stating his view of the religious educational task.[88]

For his part, Coe contends that human personality is rooted in the depths of reality. By this he seems to mean that human personality manifests an interfusion with God, and has a quality which may best be described as "sacred." Coe theorizes that at their early stage of development human beings are persons more in potentiality than in fact. The human being's journey to personhood is achieved primarily through self-affirmative participation in valuation acts. Consequently, the worth of human beings as persons (based on and arising out of the underlying, pervasive principle of continuous creation) is inherent in the Christian ideal. Therefore, development of a proper attitude toward the inexhaustible worth of persons might well lead to a re-created Christian education which would at least aim "to awaken personality and help it to rich self-activity in a society of persons."[89] This kind of re-created Christian education, Coe maintains, would not present life's problems as solved; conversely, it would require all persons to take their part in a risky, mountainously difficult adventure through participation with God in the re-creation of a moral order—a society of persons bound together in lively good will.[90] Coe succinctly defines Christian education from this personalist perspective as: ". . . the systematic, critical examination and reconstruction of relations between persons, guided by Jesus' assumption that persons are of infinite worth, and by the hypothesis of the existence of God, the Great Valuer of Persons."[91]

The student's responsibility to society

The social-cultural concept of salvation lays upon religious education the heavy burden of enabling the student to participate in the reconstruction of an ideal society. Through this entering into the turmoil of social endeavor (and thus suffering with God) the student loses his individuality, but gains life. However, this activity in humanity's struggle toward a present salvation is not mere involvement in mass action; it is, rather, responsible participation in a deliberative group. This deliberative participation in a group, in turn, leads to an effective regard for one another in such a way that the individual is disengaged from the mass. Thus conceived, social education ultimately individualizes men, at least theoretically.[92]

The Environment

Social-cultural theorists appear to understand and appreciate the impact of the environment upon religious education. However, the deliberate control of the environment as a specific variable in religious educational practice is not a typical characteristic of this approach. Sophia Lyon Fahs asserts that "all life, all existence" is appropriate resource material for religious education. It is only in a very general sense that Fahs proposes to use environment as a religious educational tool. "The early lilacs," "the mire of the pond-side," and "the mother at home" are actually only samples from the environment.[93]

George Coe concerns himself with the religious educational effects of societal surroundings — albeit, a somewhat modified use of the environmental notion. He remarks, for example, upon the "social inheritance" of the American child which includes such environmental factors as sights and sounds from the street, amusements, business and social customs, home conditions, and the influence of every "man way" that he meets. Coe, concerned with potential negative religious educational effects stemming from the environment, suggests that religious educationists need to be more aware of the reasons why efforts to teach religion are so often nullified by the student's contact with life. He argues that education, in the technical sense, consists in deliberately controlling social and environmental elements. For this reason, Coe proposes a more rigorous analysis of social and environmental effects. His conceptualization and treatment of environment as a variable in religious education is so broad, however, as to be of limited practical use to the work-a-day religion teacher in a parish setting.[94]

William Clayton Bower maintains that if it can be accepted that personality is the result of experiences that persons have it logically follows that the way to control the development of personality (which he regards as the central concern of religious education) is to control the quality and direction of experience. Experience, by his definition, derives from the interaction of the growing person ("a forthreaching organism") on one hand and a stimulating, dynamic, and expanding environment (consisting of nature, society, culture, and cosmic reality) on the other. Thus, Bower recognizes environment as a significant, but largely uncontrollable, factor in religious education. Because he perceives education to proceed experimentally in a scientific fashion, one might say that environment, for Bower, is a dependent variable; experience, being controllable, is an independent variable.[95]

Evaluation

The pragmatic philosophical underpinnings of the social-cultural theoretical approach to religious education insure its orientation toward efficiency, its setting of standards, and its development of evaluative measures. Representative social-cultural theorists typically believe that the church is directly responsible to society; they therefore hold that it should be held accountable for the results secured from its educational agencies. Religious processes and practices that survive in the church, according to this viewpoint, must demonstrate their inherent right to a place in the scheme of things by surviving rigorous scientific assessment. For this reason, it is not surprising that some social-cultural theorists manifest an interest in knowing "the dollar and person costs" of religious educational practices as tested against the results of these practices in terms of students equipped for religious, socially responsible living. "Measure, evaluate, test — these are the watchwords of the present-day spirit, and they will inevitably be applied to the church and its methods in common with other forms of social enterprise."[96]

Among the underlying reasons for careful evaluation in religious education that have been noted by social-culturally oriented religious educationists are: (1) evaluation leads to a clarified view of the elements in a religious educational situation; (2) evaluation promotes reflective thinking; (3) evaluation creates a basis for higher forms of value by which religious educationists may gain insights concerning the urgent demands that are laid upon them in the modern world; and (4) evaluation gives rise to knowledge that could not otherwise be gained.[97]

Evaluation of learning outcomes

Student learning outcomes are the immediate focus of evaluative procedures that have been proposed by social-cultural educationists. This is especially so in the case of observable qualitative change in the student's lived life as a result of his religious education. George Herbert Betts contends that the teacher must not simply evaluate his teaching upon the basis of how many facts have been acquired by the student because the real issue is how much effect his teaching has had upon the life, character, and conduct of the student. The final test of teaching, Betts argues, is whether the student (as a result of religious instruction) actually lives differently here and now in his home, school, church, and community.[98] Similarly, William Clayton Bower asserts that Christian education is put to the test by whether or not growing persons and groups of persons have been helped by their religious educational experience both to achieve loyalty to Christ and to a Christian quality of life.[99] George Coe states that: "For teachers of the Christian religion the universal guide and test is, Am I helping my pupils grow in the personal or ethical-love way of dealing both with themselves and with others whose lives they touch? . . . Am I helping them master the conditions of efficient good-will by using the methods of science with reference to all facts involved, whether facts of history, of external nature, or of the mind of man?"[100]

Supervision of religious education

There is a tendency among social-cultural theorists to connect evaluation of religious education, especially in parish settings, with the supervisory function. Ernest Chave, for example, remarks that every phase of supervision involves some aspect of testing or measuring.[101] George Coe suggests that it is a supervisory responsibility both to develop standards of educational efficiency for every religious educational office and to develop tests of educational efficiency.[102] (A standard is a goal or point that the teacher sets out to reach in a given time; a test is a means of measuring the progress toward this goal.) Coe believes that standards of whatever sort are likely to remain somewhat hazy until appropriate tests are devised.[103]

Social-culturally oriented literature contains many examples of tests for measuring religious educational progress along a number of axes. Chave's book, *Supervision of Religious Education,* for example, extensively discusses religious educational applications for such test measurement instruments as: (1) questionnaires, (2) analytic schedules, (3) rating scales, (4) objective type tests, (5) attitude scales, and (6) conduct tests.[104]

The scientific method

Social-cultural theorists are unanimous in their faith that the scientific method "which has been employed with such satisfactory results in the natural, social, and educational sciences"[105] may be fruitfully employed as a fundamental method in religious education. William Clayton Bower, after commenting upon the uncriticized and untested nature of traditional theological modes of religious education, asserts that: ". . . the profound movements that are sweeping through the educational work of the modern church and are effecting its complete reconstruction are, for the most part, the result of the scientific spirit. Under its influence the nature of religious behavior and its control are being studied, the genetic development of religious experience is being charted, the materials of religious instruction are undergoing organization, a technique of method is being worked out, the conditions of teaching are being standardized, and teachers are being scientifically trained for the task of directing the development of the religious life of the young."[106]

The application of the scientific method to religious education, according to George Coe, may best be accomplished by the adoption of personal attitudes in harmony with the scientific ideal rather than by mere slavish attention to details of scientific technique. He gives six propositions to indicate the kinds of readiness and the kinds of self-judgment that are involved in applying scientific procedures to religious educational settings: (1) the scientific method is characterized by a spirit of intellectual cooperation—the scientist acts freely as an individual, but he is also sensitive to the free acts of others; (2) in scientific work there are no foreigners, social classes, or hierarchical prerogatives, because competence is the credential; (3) the scientific spirit involves eagerness to learn, not to tell someone else what is on one's mind; (4) while every sort of logical procedure is to be respected, particular reliance is placed upon observed fact (hence, a penchant for measurement); (5) causal relations are sought by the characteristic scientific use of hypothesis, experiment, and statistical analysis; and (6) in the scientific method there is no orthodoxy except to scientific principles—the fellowship of scientific minds rests upon a common understanding of procedure and not upon a common conclusion.[107]

Notes for Chapter III

1. These again are hypothetical criteria derived from a reading of the literature.

2. Austen K. De Blois, "The Value to the Minister of the Study of Religious Education," *Religious Education*, I (June, 1906), pp. 42-46.

3. Harrison S. Elliott, *Can Religious Education Be Christian?* (New York: Macmillan, 1940), pp. 3-4.

4. Wayne R. Rood, *Understanding Christian Education* (Nashville: Abingdon, 1970), p. 41.

5. George Albert Coe, "Religious Education and General Education," *Religious Education*, XII (April, 1917), p. 123.

6. Jean-Jacques Rousseau, *Emile; ou, de l'éducation* (Paris: Garnier, 1961), p. 3. Translation mine.

7. See, for example, Michael Heafford, *Pestalozzi: His Thought and Its Relevance for Today* (London: Methuen, 1967), especially pp. 39-78.

8. Friedrich Froebel, *The Education of Man*, translated and annotated by W. N. Hailmann (New York: Appleton, 1905), especially pp. 1-36.

9. Horace Bushnell, *Christian Nurture* (New Haven: Yale University Press, 1967).

10. *Ibid.*, p. 4.

11. A. J. Wm. Myers, *Horace Bushnell and Religious Education* (Boston: Manthorne & Burrack, 1937), p. 144.

12. Wayne R. Rood, *Understanding Christian Education*, pp. 10-84; and A. J. Wm. Myers, *Horace Bushnell and Religious Education*.

13. *Ibid.*, 123-147.

14. Wayne R. Rood, *Understanding Christian Education*, pp. 92-138; also Dominique Parodi, "Knowledge and Action in Dewey's Philosophy," translated by Walter Geiske, in Paul Arthur Shilpp, editor, *The Philosophy of John Dewey* (New York: Tudor, 1951), pp. 229-242; also J. Donald Butler, *Religious Education: The Foundations and Practice of Nurture* (New York: Harper & Row, 1962), pp. 108-110.

15. For an excellent treatment of this topic, see Lawrence A. Cremin, *The Transformation of the School; Progressivism in American Education, 1876-1957* (New York: Knopf, 1961), pp. 115-117, 234-250.

16. See J. Donald Butler, *Religious Education: The Foundations and Practice of Nurture*, pp. 107-108; and Lawrence A. Cremin, *The Transformation of the School*, especially pp. vii-ix, 243-245.

17. The religious education movement took data and methodology from several scientific disciplines and applied them to problems in religious education. This movement had its concretization in the Religious Education Association, but the Association and the movement are usually referred to separately in the literature. See, for example, Harrison S. Elliott, *Can Religious Education Be Christian?* pp. 1-11; and J. Donald Butler, *Religious Education: The Foundations and Practice of Nurture*, pp. 113-121.

18. John Dewey, "Religious Education as Conditioned by Modern Psychology and Pedagogy," in *The Proceedings of the First Convention of the Religious Education Association* (Chicago, 1903), pp. 60-66.

19. George Albert Coe, "Religious Education as a Part of General Education," in *The Proceedings of the First Convention of the Religious Education Association*, pp. 44-52.

20. "The Purpose of the Association," *Religious Education*, I (April, 1906), p. 2.

21. George Albert Coe, *A Social Theory of Religious Education* (New York: Scribner's, 1917).

22. George Albert Coe, *What Is Christian Education?* (New York: Scribners, 1929), p. 23.

23. George Albert Coe, *A Social Theory of Religious Education*, pp. 13-37.

24. William Clayton Bower, *The Curriculum of Religious Education* (New York: Scribner's, 1925).

25. William Clayton Bower, *A Survey of Religious Education in the Local Church* (Chicago: University of Chicago Press, 1919).

26. William Clayton Bower, *Moral and Spiritual Values in Education* (Lexington, Kentucky: University of Kentucky Press, 1952).

27. Ernest J. Chave, *A Functional Approach to Religious Education* (Chicago: University of Chicago Press, 1947).

28. James D. Smart, *The Teaching Ministry of the Church: An Examination of the Basic Principles of Christian Education* (Philadelphia: Westminster, 1954), pp. 59-61.

29. Ernest J. Chave, *A Functional Approach to Religious Education*, especially pp. 1-16.

30. Sophia Lyon Fahs, *Today's Children and Yesterday's Heritage* (Boston: Beacon, 1952).

31. George Herbert Betts, *How to Teach Religion: Principles and Methods* (New York: Abingdon, 1919).

32. George Albert Coe, "The Idea of God," *Religious Education*, VI (June, 1911), p. 178.

33. Ernest J. Chave, *A Functional Approach to Religious Education*, p. 3.

34. Sophia Lyon Fahs, "Changes Necessary in Elementary Religious Education Due to Conflicts Between Science and Religion," *Religious Education* XXIII (April, 1928), p. 333.

35. See George Albert Coe, *What Is Christian Education?* p. 31.

36. *Ibid.*

37. William Clayton Bower, *Character Through Creative Experience*, p. 13.

38. George Albert Coe, *A Social Theory of Religious Education*, p. 6.

39. Sophia Lyon Fahs, *Today's Children and Yesterday's Heritage*, pp. 152-153.

40. George Albert Coe, *A Social Theory of Religious Education*, pp. 383-392; also *What Is Christian Education?* pp. 240-262; also William Clayton Bower, *Moral and Spiritual Values in Education*, especially p. 10.

41. William Clayton Bower, *The Curriculum of Religious Education* (New York: Scribner's, 1928), pp. 226-233; and George Albert Coe, "Virtue and the Virtues," *Religious Education*, VI (January, 1912), p. 485.

42. George Albert Coe, *A Social Theory of Religious Education*, p. 55.

43. *Ibid.*, p. 53.

44. *Ibid.*, pp. 55-57.

45. *Ibid.*, pp. 57-59.

46. *Ibid.*, especially p. 41.

47. William Clayton Bower, *Christ and Christian Education*, pp. 38-39. A more extensive treatment of aim by the same author may be found in *Religious Education in the Modern Church* (St. Louis: Bethany, 1929) pp. 28-56.

48. Ernest J. Chave, *A Functional Approach to Religious Education*, especially pp. 17-34. Chave elaborates upon these functional categories throughout the remainder of the book.

49. *Ibid.*, p. 21.

50. George Herbert Betts, *How to Teach Religion*, p. 43.

51. *Ibid.*

52. *Ibid.*, especially p. 47.

53. Sophia Lyon Fahs, *Today's Children and Yesterday's Heritage*, pp. 176-197; and William Clayton Bower, *Religious Education in the Modern Church*, especially p. 101.

54. George Albert Coe, *What Is Christian Education?* p. 46.

55. *Ibid.*, pp. 46-59. Sophia Lyon Fahs contends that beliefs held primarily because they were once revealed may become a factor in creating the opposite kinds of attitudes to those which religious

leaders usually intend to inculcate; see *Today's Children and Yesterday's Heritage,* pp. 22-29, especially p. 25.

56. See, for example, George Herbert Betts, *How to Teach Religion,* p. 38.

57. Ernest J. Chave, *A Functional Approach to Religious Education,* p. 2.

58. George Albert Coe, *A Social Theory of Religious Education,* p. 67.

59. William Clayton Bower, *Religious Education in the Modern Church,* pp. 101-123; Sophia Lyon Fahs, *Today's Children and Yesterday's Heritage,* pp. 15-30; and Ernest J. Chave, *A Functional Approach to Religious Education,* pp. 1-16.

60. George Albert Coe, *A Social Theory of Religious Education,* pp. 74-84 and 97-116.

61. *Ibid.,* pp. 18-24; and Sophia Lyon Fahs, *Today's Children and Yesterday's Heritage,* pp. 176-197.

62. William Clayton Bower, *Religious Education in the Modern Church,* pp. 115-121.

63. *Ibid.,* p. 120.

64. George Herbert Betts, *How to Teach Religion,* pp. 48-57.

65. On this particular matter Sophia Lyon Fahs is especially clear; see *Today's Children and Yesterday's Heritage,* p. 76.

66. George Albert Coe, *A Social Theory of Religious Education,* pp. 113-116.

67. *Ibid.,* pp. 19, 29, 65. Also see William Clayton Bower, *Religious Education in the Modern Church,* pp. 133-137; and Sophia Lyon Fahs, *Today's Children and Yesterday's Heritage,* especially p. 156.

68. George Albert Coe, *A Social Theory of Religious Education,* p. 65.

69. Ernest J. Chave, *Supervision of Religious Education* (Chicago: University of Chicago Press, 1931), p. 166.

70. George Albert Coe, *Education in Religion and Morals* (New York: Revell, 1904), pp. 310-311.

71. George Albert Coe, *A Social Theory of Religious Education,* pp. 270-273.

72. Ernest J. Chave, *The Supervision of Religious Education,* p. 2.

73. *Ibid.,* p. 24.

74. George Albert Coe, *A Social Theory of Religious Education*, pp. 235-236.

75. Ernest J. Chave, *A Functional Approach to Religious Education*, p. 141.

76. William Clayton Bower, *Moral and Spiritual Values in Education*, p. 41.

77. George Albert Coe, *A Social Theory of Religious Education*, pp. 28-30; also William Clayton Bower, *Religious Education in the Modern Church*, pp. 167-186.

78. George Albert Coe, *A Social Theory of Religious Education*, pp. 28-30.

79. William Clayton Bower, *Religious Education in the Modern Church*, p. 186.

80. William Clayton Bower, *Character Through Creative Experience* (Chicago: University of Chicago Press, 1930), pp. 107-270, especially pp. 107-123.

81. George Albert Coe, *A Social Theory of Religious Education*, pp. 23-24.

82. Several social-cultural theorists, notably Sophia Lyon Fahs, appear to have young children in mind when they refer to the student.

83. George Albert Coe, "Religious Education as a Part of General Education," *The Proceedings of the First Convention of the Religious Education Association* (Chicago, 1903), p. 45.

84. William Clayton Bower, *Moral and Spiritual Values in Education*, p. 39.

85. Sophia Lyon Fahs, *Today's Children and Yesterday's Heritage*, pp. 31-46.

86. George Albert Coe, *Education in Religion and Morals*, pp. 33-64; and George Herbert Betts, *How to Teach Religion*, pp. 30-40.

87. William Clayton Bower, *Moral and Spiritual Values in Education*, p. 47.

88. *Ibid.*, pp. 39-47.

89. George Albert Coe, *What Is Christian Education?* p. 68.

90. *Ibid.*, pp. 60-128.

91. George Albert Coe, *What Is Christian Education?* p. 296.

92. George Albert Coe, *A Social Theory of Religious Education*, pp. 6, 38-40, 56.

93. Sophia Lyon Fahs, *Today's Children and Yesterday's Heritage*, pp. 176-178.

94. George Albert Coe, *A Social Theory of Religious Education*, pp. 13-15.

95. William Clayton Bower, *Moral and Spiritual Values in Education*, especially pp. 48-60.

96. On these matters, see George Herbert Betts, *The New Program of Religious Education* (New York: Abingdon, 1921), p. 14; also George Albert Coe, *The Spiritual Life: Studies in the Science of Religion* (New York: Eaton & Mains, 1900), especially p. 5; and *A Social Theory of Religious Education*, p. 36.

97. William Clayton Bower, *The Curriculum of Religious Education*, pp. 99-119.

98. George Herbert Betts, *How to Teach Religion*, pp. 39-40, 91.

99. William Clayton Bower, *Christ and Christian Education* (New York: Abingdon-Cokesbury, 1943), p. 38.

100. George Albert Coe, *What Is Christian Education?* p. 178.

101. Ernest J. Chave, *Supervision of Religious Education*, p. 305.

102. George Albert Coe, *A Social Theory of Religious Education*, pp. 238-239.

103. *Ibid.*, pp. 239-240.

104. Ernest J. Chave, *Supervision of Religious Education*, pp. 305-333.

105. See William Clayton Bower, *A Survey of Religious Education in the Local Church*, p. 13.

106. William Clayton Bower, *The Educational Task of the Local Church* (St. Louis: Front Rank Press, 1921), p. 114.

107. George Albert Coe, *What Is Christian Education?* pp. 136-140.

Chapter IV

The Contemporary Theological Theoretical Approach to Religious Education

CRITERIA FOR THE CONTEMPORARY THEOLOGICAL APPROACH

The contemporary theological approach to theorizing about religious education is delineated by the following criteria. *First,* theological conceptualizations, a usual feature of which is a recognition of the present continuing revelatory activity of God, are normative for all decisions relative to religious educational theory and practice. Revelation, whether past or present, is typically perceived to have an experiential quality. The Bible is understood to be a record of revelation, but not necessarily revelatory in and of itself. *Second,* religious education aims both to establish individuals in a right relationship with God within the revelatory fellowship of the church[1] and to educate them for responsible, intelligent, adult Christian living. *Third,* the teacher's task is to enter into a communal relationship with students and guide them in their growth within themselves, toward God, and toward other persons. *Fourth,* the student's spiritual life is fostered and sustained by the educational ministry of the church.[2]

Because contemporary theological theorists tend to be highly speculative and because they represent a rather wide range of theological and educational commitments, the four above mentioned characteristics of this approach must be considered quite tentative. However, these theorists appear to be essentially united in (1) their opposition to the optimistic brand of liberal theology espoused by social-cultural theorists, (2) their recognition that man is in need of redemption, and (3) their commitment to the position that the Christian community is the locus of religious life and education. In addition, some form of participatory relationship in the community of Christians is a usual feature of the religious education practices advocated by contemporary theological theorists.

ANTECEDENTS TO THE CONTEMPORARY THEOLOGICAL APPROACH

The antecedents to the contemporary theological approach are much the same as the antecedents to the social-cultural approach, even though the contemporary theological approach represents a distinct transition from a social to a theological emphasis in theorizing about religious education. Thus, for example, the thought of Johann Pestalozzi, John Dewey, and, most especially, Horace Bushnell has had a considerable influence upon the theoretical viewpoint of both the social-cultural theorists and the contemporary theological theorists. It might also be noted that a majority of the influential theorists of both schools of thought have been active members of the Religious Education Association and that they have regularly contributed scholarly articles to its official journal, *Religious Education.*

The above mentioned transition from a social to a theological emphasis in religious education seems to have had its roots in the depression period of the 1930's. The optimistic religious education programs that had been developed and launched under the tenets of the social-cultural approach lost their momentum — and their optimism — when the economic situation of this period forced a retrenchment in many of these programs. During this period of program retrenchment (roughly the decade of the 1930's), powerful currents of theological thought were generated by the impact of works such as Karl Barth's *Der Römerbrief* (1919)[3] and Reinhold Niebuhr's *Moral Man and Immoral Society* (1932).[4] These and other works of similar import influenced some religious educational leaders to engage in a theological reevaluation of the theoretical foundations of the prevailing social-culturally oriented religious educational practices. One focal point of this reevaluation was the optimistic doctrine of man which had been a principal underpinning of the theories that molded the religious educational scene during the earlier decades of the twentieth century.[5]

By the early 1940's it was evident that this revival of theological interest had gained sufficient strength to influence the climate of the religious education scene in America. Harrison S. Elliott was among the first religious educationists to present a clear analysis of this changing situation. His *Can Religious Education Be Christian?* states the issues confronting the field at the beginning of the decade of the 1940's: "There has been an increasing tendency in Protestant churches to return to the historical formulations of the Christian religion and to repudiate the adjustments which had been made under the influence of modern scientific and social developments."[6] Elliott personally rejected the tendency to return to what he considered to be an inadequate "neo-orthodox" version of Christianity and the authoritarian approach to religious education which he believed would grow out of it. He opted for a continuation of the social-cultural variety of religious education with its emphasis upon human responsibility to discover and to pursue solutions for the problems of the world.[7]

H. Shelton Smith's *Faith and Nurture* (1941),[8] which expressed a point of view diametrically opposite to that of *Can Religious Education Be Christian?* appears to have played a significant part in opening the way for the revival of a distinctly theological approach to religious educational theory.[9] Smith contended that the emergence of post-liberal patterns of religious thought which challenged the former (social-cultural) concepts of Christian nurture had forced the following question upon religious educationists: "Shall Protestant nurture realign its theological foundations with the newer currents of Christian thought, or shall it resist those currents and merely reaffirm its faith in traditional liberalism?"[10] Although Smith's sentiments quite obviously favored this realignment of religious education with the newer theological currents, *Faith and Nurture* was largely devoted to "unsparing criticism" of the theoretical bases of religious education as it was conceptualized by the school of thought represented by George Coe, William Clayton Bower, and Sophia Lyon Fahs. Smith thus left the work of religious educational realignment to others.

A landmark, of sorts, in the theological realignment proposed by Smith resulted from the establishment of a committee of the International Council of Religious Education in 1944.

Among other responsibilities which included, in effect, surveying the entire field of religious education, this committee was charged with the specific responsibility of examining "the need of a considered statement as to the place of theological and other concepts in Christian education."[11] The major report of this committee, edited by Paul Vieth, was published in 1947 as *The Church and Christian Education*.[12] Even though this report did not bring about a theological consensus within the field of religious education, *The Church and Christian Education* does incorporate foundational theological elements that are described by James Smart as being "far removed from the optimistic liberalism of Coe or Chave."[13] Sara Little identifies this report as the beginning of a clearly discernible theological emphasis in religious education which is distinctive enough to be termed a movement.[14]

REPRESENTATIVE CONTEMPORARY THEOLOGICAL THEORISTS

Randolph Crump Miller, a longtime editor of *Religious Education* and a leading educator of persons preparing for professional positions in the field of religious education, is possibly the most influential theorist of the contemporary theological school of thought. His stated position that "Christian theology is the primary source of Christian educational theory and procedure" seems to fall well within the compass of the contemporary theological approach. Miller's most fundamental contribution to the development of the contemporary theological approach to theory is probably his 1950 publication, *The Clue to Christian Education*.[15] This book was profoundly influenced by H. Shelton Smith's *Faith and Nurture*. An encapsulation of Miller's viewpoint is that: "The clue to Christian education is the rediscovery of a relevant theology which will bridge the gap between content and method, providing the background and perspective of Christian truth by which the best methods and content will be used as tools to bring the learners into the right relationship with the living God who is revealed to us in Jesus Christ, using the guidance of parents and the fellowship of life in the church as the environment in which Christian nurture will take place."[16]

A second religious educationist whose theoretical position

seems to be described by the criteria of the contemporary theological approach is Lewis Sherrill. His book, *The Gift of Power* (1955),[17] was specifically intended to be a contribution to that theorizing about religious education which he perceived to be "emerging as a result of the plight of modern man, and the new currents of religious and psychological thought concerning it."[18] Sherrill professes to be in search of a Christian education in which the core educational process is a revelatory encounter between God as self and man as self. He believes that the relevance of such a revelatory education process is that it will meet man's existing spiritual and psychological needs as well as call forth his capacities as a person. The locus of this kind of religious education is the Christian community (church) in which both God and men participate in an intricate web of relationships. Theoretically, according to Sherrill, religious education "is the attempt, ordinarily by members of the Christian community, to participate in and to guide the changes which take place in persons in their relationships with God, with the church, with other persons, with the physical world, and with oneself."[19]

The church is also a key element in James Smart's attempt to develop a viable, ecumenically Christian solution to the theoretical and practical problems of religious education. He argues that religious education, in the Christian sense, can only be understood against the background of the New Testament concepts of "God" and "church." Since the church is "the fellowship of those persons to whom God is making himself known," Smart theorizes that it is the proper focal point of all religious educational activity.[20] His major contributions to religious educational theory are *The Teaching Ministry of the Church* (1954)[21] and *The Creed in Christian Teaching* (1962).[22]

The Roman Catholic theologian and religious educational thinker, Gabriel Moran, seems to hold to a theoretical position on religious education which is in basic agreement with the criteria of the contemporary theological approach. Moran, who contends that religious educational theory flows out of theology, appears to be somewhat of a theoretical adventurer who casts his searchlight of speculative interest upon mountain peaks of possibility. He centers his attention on revelation which he has defined as being "a personal communion of knowledge, an interrelationship of God and the individual within a believing community."[23] Moran defends the notion that religious education is a revelationally active process in which the teacher's role "is to set students on the road toward understanding by helping them to use their intelligences creatively, originally, and constructively."[24] Religious education, then, is not an indoctrinational process in which children are prepared to be good members of a certain religious communion; rather, it is a preparation for adult participation in life as it flows into the future.[25] Of Moran's several books, *Catechesis of Revelation* (1966),[26] *Vision and Tactics* (1968),[27] and *Design for Religion* (1970)[28] are particularly relevant to this investigation.[29]

Although the writings of Miller, Sherrill, Smart, and Moran have been selected as the major representative literature of the contemporary theological approach to religious education, the writings of several other influential theorists, such as D. Campbell Wyckoff, Sara Little, Iris Cully, and Howard Grimes, appear to express a similar viewpoint. Accordingly, these latter writings also have been utilized in this study.

ANALYSIS OF THE CONTEMPORARY
THEOLOGICAL APPROACH

The Aim

Genesis of aim

The development of religious educational aims for advocates of the contemporary theological approach is dependent upon responsible theological interpretation of relevant information gleaned from such sources as the Bible, the church's life, the culture, and the human situation. The aims of this approach thus reflect an attempt on the part of its theorists to give due recognition to cultural changes while continuing in the spirit of biblical tradition. To this end, Randolph Crump Miller suggests that religious education must be grounded in a theology which recognizes God as the center and goal of its educational process.[30]

For several contemporary theologically oriented theorists the concept of continuing revelation is a vital element in the evolution of religious educational aims. Gabriel Moran, for example, strongly supports the position that revelation not only is a personal, here-and-now relationship being participated in by both God and man but that a commitment to this theological viewpoint is indispensable to the improvement of religious education.[31] In a similar vein, Lewis Sherrill states that: "... when man encounters the Self-revealing God he is confronted ... by a Person who offers himself to us in love and judgment, and calls upon us to give ourselves a living sacrifice in response. It is a matter of personal communion. If this is the core of revelation, so must it be the core of Christian education."[32]

Focus of aim

In contrast both with traditional theological aims which focus upon the transmission of a salvific message and with social-cultural aims which focus upon the development of an idealized social order, contemporary theological religious educational aims are typically focused in the church and in its corporate life. Thus James Smart affirms that the purposes of religious education from the Christian perspective cannot be understood apart from a clear understanding of the church which came into being as a consequence of God's breaking into our world in Jesus Christ.[33] With similar import, Randolph Crump Miller states that: "The main task is to teach the truth about God, with all the implications arising from God's nature and activity, in such a way that the learner will accept Jesus Christ as Lord and Savior, will become a member of the Body of Christ, and will live in the Christian way."[34] Within the scope of aims which are focused in the church, contemporary theological theorists have concerned themselves with several specific religious educational objectives, namely: personal growth, intellectual growth, biblical understanding, and training for effective participation in the life of the church.

Personal growth and development within the fellowship of the church is regarded by a number of contemporary theological theorists as a key focal point of religious educational aim. The religious educational process, it is theorized, should aim both to lead individuals into a living encounter with God and to provide spiritual support for them as they grow toward wholeness through living out the meaning of this encounter. Thus Randolph Crump Miller asserts that a major purpose of religious education is to make man whole through the establishment of secure relationships among persons within a dynamic Christian community in which there is also a continuing encounter with God and an organic connection with the environment.[35] Lewis Sherrill likewise touches directly upon this matter in what is possibly his best known statement of religious educational aim: ". . . that persons might be drawn into the kingdom of God; that they might attain increasing self-understanding and self-knowledge and an increasing realization of their own potentialities; and that they might sustain the relationships and responsibilities of life as children of God."[36]

The *intellectual growth* of individual Christians is looked upon by many contemporary theological theorists as a valid, albeit often neglected, aim of religious education. Gabriel Moran takes for granted that the proper business of religious education is not the divine task of saving students, but it is, rather, "the human task of freeing men for life in the Spirit by awakening intelligence and freedom."[37] A similar viewpoint is taken by J. Gordon Chamberlin, who suggests that religious education has sometimes been used simply as a tool to "press virtue into young sinners" instead of pressing toward the also well-founded objective of educating Christians.[38]

Contemporary theological theorists usually hold that a principal function of the educational work of the church is, or at least ought to be, to introduce persons to the Bible. This biblical introduction, it is acknowledged, must go well beyond either the mere transmission of information about the Bible or the rote memorization of biblical passages; it must promote an *understanding of the Bible* in terms of its continuing relevant message. The Bible, then, is considered to be worth knowing in and of itself because it is the primary written witness to revelation, it is the basic source of Christian theology, and its principles provide the potential solutions to many of mankind's problems. In addition, it has been theorized that a knowledge of the Bible will "prepare the way for men to receive God and to respond to him in the present."[39]

The education and training of persons within the church to be the church is another aspect of religious educational aim commonly mentioned among contemporary theological theorists. This education for the "life in Christ" is said to involve a remaking, renewing, transforming process that not only sets it off from other forms of education but makes it specifically Christian. The ultimate aim of religious education, from this viewpoint, is that the living Christ will take hold of all of life through the witness and functional ministry of an educated and committed church. Lewis Sherrill declared that this kind of transforming education, which is not fully possible outside of the Christian community, takes place naturally within the fellowship of the Christian community as God confronts man in the continuing redemptive disclosure of himself.[40] In a similar spirit, but using different imagery, James Smart summarizes his approach to the goals of religious education: "Christian education exists because the life that came into the world in Jesus Christ demands a human channel of communication that it may reach an ever-widening circle of men, women, and children, and become their life. The aim of Christian teaching is to widen and deepen that human channel, to help forward the growth and enrichment of the human fellowship, through which Jesus Christ moves ever afresh into the life of the world to redeem mankind."[41]

Scope of aim

The scope of religious educational aims advanced by contemporary theological theorists is broadened by the sensitivity of these theorists to changing cultural conditions and by the high value that many of them place upon individual freedom. This broadened scope of religious educational aim contributes to a certain admitted fuzziness and lack of specificity in many contemporary theologically oriented statements of aim. Definite religious educational aims, such as are suitable to an era of unchanging religious traditions (in which it is rather certain that students will stay with the particular tradition and continue to view life from that tradition's perspective), are not considered feasible in the everchanging contemporary society. D. Campbell Wyckoff remarks that the aim of religious education might well be put in the following way: ". . . that we may become persons who see things as they are and who come to grips with life."[42] Wyckoff's contention is that the factors which distinguish a genuinely Christian education from technical, general, and moral education (namely that it ministers to the need for the life transformed by God and guided by the Holy Spirit) may be most effectively developed through the reality of "seeing things as they are" and through the action involved in "coming to grips with life" in the context of this reality.[43] J. Gordon Chamberlin also sets forth the idea that the aims of religious education must be allowed to change as the student's worldview and environment change. Chamberlin proposes the concept of "no static ends" as a means of eventually attaining "the educated person who has engaged in a self-conscious reexamination of his views on the meaning of existence, who has been confronted by a competent interpretation of the Christian faith, and who accepts his responsibility for the many decisions of his life in the light of his education."[44]

Lewis Sherrill seeks to avoid what he perceives to be the peril of having religious educational aims that are so specific that religious educators are drawn into the unhappy business of trying to predetermine the behavior of students. Sherrill suggests that one means of avoiding this peril is to keep the presently existing self of the student at the center of religious educational concern. He believes that the principal educational changes occur during the revelation encounter which takes place within the depths of the student as he is confronted with the self-revealing God. The Christian life of the student, then, is not a living out of the rules that have been attached in some manipulatory fashion to the periphery of the self; instead, it is the living response to the God who offers himself to us in love, as well as in judgment.[45]

Gabriel Moran proposes that the scope of religious educational aim ought also to include the freedom of students. He holds that freedom can no longer be a side issue in religious educational aim because of the rising consciousness which has become a fact of modern life. To include the giving of freedom within the scope of religious educational aim, Moran believes, would give recognition to the potential for a more revelationally active kind of Christianity. He affirms that Christianity could in this way offer "the incentive to open understanding and freedom to the boundless reality of personal value and communal love."[46]

The scope of religious educational aims as they are commonly conceived by contemporary theological theorists seems to be so broad, so noble, and so ultimately "boundless" as to insure that these aims will be of little practical use in either the planning of classroom educational process or in determining its actual consequences. Rather than clarifying the teaching task, it appears that such broad aims might well contribute a certain vagueness in the perceived purposes for the teaching of religion.

Social and moral dimensions of aim

Although religious educational aim for theorists who espouse the contemporary theological viewpoint tends to be focused in the church and in the nurture of the Christian's personal life, these theorists are cognizant of social and moral responsibilities encumbent upon the church and upon Christians. Randolph Crump Miller, for example, contends that the very relevance of the Christian faith depends upon the living response of the Christian to this faith in Jesus Christ. This living response involves, in the first place, discovering the implications of the Christian faith and, in the second place, living out these implications either through participation in social change or in some other ministry of the church to the world.[47] D. Campbell Wyckoff suggests that beyond the aim of nurturing the Christian life there is the aim of a life to be lived and a character to be built. Wyckoff finds three focuses to this aspect of religious educational aim, namely that Christian education may (1) be effective in helping persons build lives of integrity, (2) help persons live lives that are socially responsible, and (3) enable persons to live lives in full recognition of God.[48] He further states that Christian education cannot claim to have achieved its ultimate aims until Christians have effected such changes in society whereby the very processes of the larger community contribute to, rather than hinder, the process of religious and Christian growth. "A church," to use Wyckoff's words, "may well state its Christian education aims in terms of such outcomes as these in the lives of its pupils: intelligent belief, Christian commitment, Christian character, churchmanship, and participation in the redemption of the community."[49]

Gabriel Moran declares that a pedagogy centered upon the personal revelation of God in the risen Christ would lead to the resolution of most of the moral and social questions upon which so much time is wasted in fruitless teaching activity. Christian morality, he believes, needs to be presented as a creative re-sponse on the part of man to the situations in which he finds himself. The moral anchor, then, would not be a list of do's and don't's, but rather one's understanding of the life, death, and resurrection of Jesus—and especially of his continual working in the church today. From Moran's viewpoint, every genuinely loving act is revelatory of God through Christ and the Spirit. Indeed, for him, such acts contain the whole of revelation. This approach to religious and moral teaching, based as it is upon a theology of continuing revelation, theoretically offers the possi-bility of a religious education which will lead to an adult level of responsible religious life. The teacher's role in an education based upon these principles and aims would be to help the student discover and develop his own potentialities so that he would become a free and responsible person, unique and creative within his own being.[50]

The mission and ministry of the church to the world seems to hold a central place in James Smart's conception of the social and moral dimensions of religious educational aim. The larger purposes of religious education, according to Smart, must be continuous with the line of development that was marked out for the church in the New Testament. The goal of religious education must be coextensive with the goal of Jesus and the apostles. This goal would demand that religion teaching aim at no less than (1) to enable God to work in the hearts of students, making of them committed disciples; (2) to produce both un-derstanding and personal faith adequate for students to main-tain a vital Christian witness in the midst of an unbelieving world; (3) to enable God to bring into being a church marked by God's presence and committed to the service of Jesus Christ "as an earthly body through which he may continue his redemption of the world"; and (4) to enable students to grow into full life and active faith in the church, thus sharing in its mission.[51]

The Content

Content corresponds with present experience

The content of religious education, according to most con-temporary theological theorists, can neither be defined in terms of an authoritative message alone nor in terms of present living alone. Although it cannot be said that these theorists have themselves arrived at a fully common theoretical viewpoint, it appears that in an overall way they are committed to an attempt to define religious educational content in such a way that it is neither disconnected from the historic Christian message nor meaningless in terms of present experience. The correspondence of content and present experience, then, is a critical factor in the contemporary theological approach to the matter of religious educational content.

This correspondence between religious educational content and present experience is conceptualized in several ways by individual theorists. Randolph Crump Miller, for example, theorizes that a twofold relationship between God and the student is at the center of the religious educational curriculum. This means, according to Miller, that the curriculum is both God-centered and experience-centered. Theology, "truth-about-God-in-relation-to-man,"[52] has both a critical and explanatory function in Miller's scheme; and, in his words, it "must be prior to the curriculum."[53] Miller states that: "The task of Christian education is not to teach theology, but to use theology as the basic tool for bringing learners into the right relationship with God in the fellowship of the Church."[54] Within the guidelines delineated by what he refers to as an "informed theology," Miller appears to agree with several other theorists who hold that teaching materials for religious education might well develop directly out of the experience of teacher and student together. He asserts that both past and presently happening experiences of teacher and student offer a solid base for bringing systematized knowledge from the past to bear upon the concerns of the present. In this way Miller develops a rationale for using biblical materials in a life-oriented religious educational program in which the student will be enabled to live meaningfully now and in the future. This kind of experientially based, theologically sound curriculum, Miller believes, will bridge the gap between content and method, truth and life, doctrine and experience. It will also enable religion teachers to "teach not so much things as the meaning of things."[55]

D. Campbell Wyckoff advances three principles which he believes may be of help to the religion teacher in dealing with this relationship between content and experience: (1) that human experience for any person is continuous; (2) that personality develops through experience; and (3) that experience may be guided and enriched. Wyckoff claims that these three principles constitute a groundwork for a unified concept of the religious educational process in which "subject matter and experience, content and experience" would be combined. Theoretically, the teacher would employ his own experience and that of the student, together with the rich truths of the Christian faith, as he directs students toward the experience of God as a central reality. This education "for the life in Christ" would include for most students (Wyckoff recognizes levels of ability) "a thoroughgoing analysis of and commitment to the Christian faith as doctrine, as teaching, and as a definitive formulation of what the life in Christ is."[56]

Religious educationists such as Lewis Sherrill and Howard Grimes who place especial importance in the church as a fellowship usually hold that the content of religious education is constituted in major part by those inner changes in persons that grow out of the interactions that take place within the Christian community. Sherrill is particularly concerned with the relationship between education and revelation. He distinguishes between *content of learning* (those changes that take place within the person as a result of his participation in a dynamic, revelationally active religious educational process) and *materials of learning* (matter presented to the student by responsible persons as a means to bring about changes). Sherrill's most intense interest seems to be concentrated upon issues related to the "deeper" levels of communication that take place within the Christian community, the scene where God redemptively reveals himself to men and where men influence one another in the responses they make to God. The Christian education growing out of this deep communication (which, it is said, can only take place to its fullest extent within the Christian community) does not lead to the accumulation of information as such, "but to the actual experience of the Person and the events with which the information deals."[57] Grimes claims that the heart of religious educational content is the creative encounter between man and man, and man and God that takes place in community.

This means that in order to convey its message of love and concern the church must become a community of love and concern.[58]

The centrality of experience is also a major premise of Gabriel Moran's religious educational theorizing. He argues that the teaching of doctrinal content must spring from, and be continuously reflected in, human life itself. According to Moran's theoretical viewpoint, nothing is more useless to a revelationally grounded religious education than the mainte- nance of a system of abstractly defined truths which sustain no supportable relationship to the real world. Moran holds that religion teachers should be much more interested in helping students know God than they are in transmitting information about God. Consequently, he suggests that debate concerning questions which surround matters of content and method is often so simplistic as to be practically meaningless. The really serious theoretical questions to which Moran thinks religious educationists should address themselves relate to the circum- stances under which any human being (religion teacher or otherwise) can help another person to know God. Moran's works on religious educational theory bear witness to his convic- tion that present experience is the pivot point of those religious educational practices which successfully lead to a revelationally vivified knowledge of God.[59]

Subject matter

Although experience is the usual center of interest for con- temporary theological theorizing about the content of religious education, there is a nearly unanimous agreement among rep- resentative theorists that subject matter relating specifically to the Christian faith must be integrated into the religious educa- tional process. Commonly mentioned sources of such subject matter include the Bible, Christian theology, church history, and stories of the church today. These specifically Christian sources of subject matter are, of course, in addition to those sources which extend as far as the experience of the race. Most contemporary theological theorists would seem likely to agree with Randolph Crump Miller that subject matter ought to be employed selectively for the specific purpose of "opening up the channels of God's grace so that men may respond in faith to the Gospel."[60] Theological considerations are usually considered determinative of that specific subject matter which is most fundamental in a given situation. In addition, individual interests, capacities, and needs are recognized as mandating the grading of subject matter.[61]

The Bible, ordinarily perceived to be a record of revelation rather than a revelation in and of itself, is considered by contemporary theological theorists to be the single most important source of subject matter for religious education. These theorists, however, unanimously reject the traditional theological notion that religious education comes about through the transmission of biblical content. James Smart, for example, castigates religious education which stops short when biblical information has been handed on, although he agrees that biblical facts need to be assimilated by students. Smart maintains that the central purpose in teaching the Bible is that God may speak through it into the lives of students who are being taught—*now*. The religion teacher's handling of the Bible, then, should be with the expectation that God will make his word come alive with the power in which it was originally spoken.[62] Lewis Sherrill has stated that introducing persons to the Bible is among the primary functions of religious education. Sherrill theorizes that the Bible, as a record of God's disclosure of himself to man, may fruitfully be used to prepare men to respond to God in the present. Accordingly, biblical subject matter is introduced into the experience of the student as a means of precipitating his personal encounter with, and response to, God. A subsidiary purpose for using biblical materials in religious education is that God's people today may become familiar with the history of God's people in the Bible. Sherrill suggests that the histories, narratives, and life stories contained in the Bible are especially appropriate for this purpose.[63]

Randolph Crump Miller is likewise committed to the view that the Bible, as a primary source of the Christian faith, has a rightful place at the center of the religious educational process. While Miller holds it to be true that the Bible is the basic authority for theology, he believes it is evident that theology is the proper guide to the meaning of the Bible. Within the guidelines determined by a responsible theology, then, Miller suggests that the religious educational task is to relate biblical concepts to those relationships that are a part of our daily lives. His major effort to accomplish this task is *Biblical Theology and Christian Education* (1956)[64] in which he formulates his biblical theology in terms of the biblical drama of redemption.[65]

Gabriel Moran, agrees with those Protestant contemporary theological theorists who hold that the Bible should have a primary role in the process of teaching religion, but he argues that it should not be confused with the whole process. Although Moran repeatedly denies that the Bible is in any sense a collection of revealed truths, he includes the biblical words within the revelatory relationship of God and man because "the revelational process could not help but have a verbal element."[66] Moran suggests that the Bible may in fact enable man to recognize revelation as it happens in the free existence of man within the present community of Christians. Although he does not advocate a program of Bible teaching, as such, Moran agrees that the scriptures, both Old and New Testament, are indispensable in teaching about Jesus Christ "who is the revelatory communion of God and man."[67]

The Teacher

One key assumption in the generally accepted contemporary theological viewpoint on teaching religion is that God participates with man in the revelationally active process of religious education. A second, closely related assumption is that responsibility for religious education, from the human side, rests with the whole church. According to typical contemporary theologically oriented theorizing, then, the religion teacher functions both in subordination to the Holy Spirit (the Great Teacher who teaches over and above humanly contrived methods) and as a representative of the church (whose members are called upon to support his teaching by their lives and witness). Thus, from this theoretical perspective, the religion teacher is neither the transmitter of an unchanging message nor is he the hopeful creator of an idealized social order; rather, he is both promotor and participant in a process through which God is revealing himself to men today.

The ideal characteristics of the contemporary theologically oriented religion teacher are most adequately summarized by Reuel Howe: *first,* he will seek to incarnate the Holy Spirit rather than to convey subject matter; *second,* he will value the student's freedom to be himself and will offer the gift of relationship to the student as he searches for the realities of the Christian faith; *third,* he will trust both the Holy Spirit and the student in the educational process; *fourth,* he will be neither anxious about methods nor too strongly committed to any individual method but will creatively use whatever methods are at this disposal according to the demands of a particular situation; and *fifth,* he will be committed to the belief that revelation occurs in person-to-person relationships, and he will speak as a person to the person of his student expecting that revelation will call forth a response.[68]

The religion teacher's qualifications

Intelligently active participation in the Christian community is looked upon by typical contemporary theological theorists as being the initial qualification for teaching religion. Some theorists, Gabriel Moran, for example, also require that the prospective teacher be willing to become personally involved in thinking through theological problems.[69] The ideal candidate for teaching religion, to use several of D. Campbell Wyckoff's standards, is a continually growing person who is becoming more competent in biblical understanding; in the Christian faith; and in active Christian service, fellowship, and worship.[70] Many contemporary theologically oriented theorists share Randolph Crump Miller's conviction that a prerequisite for Christian teaching is an enthusiasm for teaching born of both a contageous commitment to the Christian religion and a loving concern for students.[71] These theorists tend to assume that the person who meets the above, very general, requirements can develop into a competent religion teacher by availing himself of the means for developing skills and spiritual sensitivities that will support his teaching ministry.

The religion teacher's training

Although there is general agreement among contemporary theorists that the training of religion teachers is an absolute necessity, these theorists can hardly be said to have succeeded in developing a consistent, well-defined theoretical base upon which to build the kind of large-scale program which could accomplish the training of an adequate number of competent teachers. Training programs conducted under the rather broadly defined tenets of this approach exhibit a theological orientation; they are typically targeted toward the teacher's (1) intellectual and spiritual growth, (2) his aquisition of appropriate educational skills, and (3) the development of his spiritual and interpersonal sensitivities.

Both James Smart and Gabriel Moran have strongly supported the view that the training of religion teachers should have a primarily, and perhaps exclusively, theological orientation. Smart charges that teacher training in church school settings has been notably weak in preparing teachers to deal with theological questions even though it has often been effective in giving them methodological skills. He contends that persons preparing to teach require the same biblical, theological, and historical grounding as persons preparing to preach. Theological error in teaching is considered quite as damaging as theological error in preaching. On the other hand, since the purpose of teaching is not merely to pour knowledge into students, Smart favors some studies which would enable the teacher to be able to guide students in their growth as Christian persons.[72] Gabriel Moran is convinced that theological inquiry must be at the heart of any training program which will have the capacity to produce the much needed, truly competent religion teachers. He theorizes that as prospective religion teachers inquire into presently significant religious and secular issues they can be brought to see beyond the distracting religious questions of the past to the main issue, namely, that God confronts man revelationally in the present. Such a theologically oriented training program, Moran believes, should result in the training of a teacher who through reading, reflection, discussion and self-engaging theologizing has gained an intellectual confidence that will enable him to give up any reliance upon religious educational content which supposedly descends from above; rather, he will discover both content and teaching methods in communion with this students who are together with him participating in God's present revelatory activity.[73]

From another perspective, D. Campbell Wyckoff puts forward the notion that teacher training should emphasize the qualities of the teacher's life as well as his teaching methods. He states: "Teacher training will seek to develop teaching skills that will give ever more effective expression to our mutual search for the Christian truth and way of life. It will stress training in the life of the spirit—not just, 'What do I do with these children?' but, 'How may I become the kind of person who can do the kind of job that needs to be done?' "[74] Wyckoff also supports the position that teacher training should include "on-the-job" training and that the teacher (particularly the volunteer) should have access to competent supervisory aid.[75]

The religion teacher's method

Revelation, conceptualized as a divine here-and-now occurrence within the Christian community, is a key element in contemporary theologically oriented theorizing about religion teaching method. Theorists committed to this approach usually believe that God through the Holy Spirit is revelationally present and actively involved in making the religion teaching process effective. Method is accordingly looked upon as a potentially dynamic vehicle of Christian revelation. Because contemporary theological theorists often hold that the Holy Spirit (who works where and when he wills) teaches above and beyond humanly contrived teaching methods, it is not surprising that they tend to discourage the teacher from placing his confidence in any particular method, or methods, of teaching religion. Nevertheless, the works of many contemporary theological theorists evince a considerable interest in method; in fact, they usually encourage the religion teacher to become proficient in a number of methods. The contemporary theologically oriented religion teacher's expertise in method, then, must of necessity include a certain, though somewhat unspecified, sensitivity to the working of the Holy Spirit, as well as to the needs of his students which will enable him to select (or as some theorists might put it, to create) an appropriate method for each given instance.

The overarching religion teaching method which flows quite naturally from the underlying theories of the contemporary theological approach is, in sum and substance, to be the church of Jesus Christ as resonating with the Holy Spirit. Thus, D. Campbell Wyckoff submits that the heart of method in teaching the Christian religion is full participation in the life of the church by living the Christian life under "experienced guidance." Each class in the church school, from Wyckoff's perspective, "*is* the church of the living Christ."[76] Therefore, the clue to method is for the church to involve every one of its children, youth, and adults in the responsibilities of maintaining a creative relationship to its living Lord.[77] Similarly, James Smart holds that the fundamental principle of Christian education is that the teaching function belongs to the very essence of the church. Recognition of this principle means, for Smart, that the work of the teacher is rooted in the ministry of the church in the same way that the work of the preacher is rooted in the ministry of the church. In his view, this recognition of the "essential nature" of the teaching function might well lead to a resolution of the uncertainties which sometimes surround the teacher and his teaching ministry within the church. Responsibility for teaching, though, does not rest solely upon the teacher; it rests upon the whole church. In the larger view of the church's teaching ministry, from this perspective, it is ultimately God who teaches. "Therefore," Smart states, "the vital function of the church and church school is not to explain all human experience, but to bring together, in a living way, the person who is confronted with the mystery of the meaning of the world and the Christian revelation of God which alone is the key to the mystery."[78]

Randolph Crump Miller likewise holds that the church is the functional center of religious educational method. He reasons that if the congregation is a vital community of the Holy Spirit it will affect all that happens in the religion classes of the local church. In particular, these classes can be transmuted into centers of fellowship, each one bearing marks of a Christian group. Miller's understanding of the process whereby a class becomes a Christian group may be summarized as follows: *first,* the Christian group begins with persons where they are, the teacher assuming initial responsibility for activities; *second,* the Christian group life starts with God, even though group members may differ in their degree of dialogue with God and in their ability to verbalize their faith; *third,* the Christian group interaction begins as the living Lord becomes a part of the encounter which takes place where two or three are gathered in his name—things may well happen within this interaction process which would not normally happen because God in

Christ moves through the Holy Spirit in a mysterious way to heal wounds, break down barriers, sustain fellowship; and *fourth,* the Christian group is ultimately created by the Holy Spirit as he establishes relationships wherein God's revelation can be shared.[79] Miller recognizes that there are no "sure-fire" methods to create this kind of group spirit and that there are dangers (a kind of conformity to the group, for example). However, he believes that the potential values outweigh the dangers because it is God who acts through the group "to provide the spiritual growth which is the gift of grace."[80]

In similar fashion, Lewis Sherrill suggests that religious education takes place primarily in the Christian community, especially in the process of interaction between persons. His concern is that methods must be conducive to enabling human selves to enter the high destiny for which they were created. The core purpose of any method, according to Sherrill's relational viewpoint, is to facilitate effective, spiritually uplifting, two-way communication between selves. If any particular method proves to be effective in accomplishing this spiritually uplifting, two-way communication, Sherrill holds it to be an appropriate method to use in Christian education. However, by way of caution, he notes that methods which prove themselves fruitful in certain situations and with certain selves may prove unfruitful in other settings and with other selves. Hence, no one method can lay claim to being *the* method for Christian education.[81]

Gabriel Moran's approach to religion teaching method is heavily influenced by his strongly held conviction that Christian revelation "is a personal communion of knowledge, an interrelationship of God and the individual within a believing community."[82] Teaching method, accordingly, does not begin with a body of curricular subject matter; it begins with persons precisely because it is among persons that revelation happens. Subject matter has its place in the religion teaching process primarily as a means of aiding in the expression and understanding of God's revelation of himself in human life. This is most fruitfully done by any method that most fully involves the student in active theologizing. Religion teaching, from Moran's perspective, has its focus in the community which is composed of students and teachers as they open themselves to the wider community of men before God. It is axiomatic, for him, that religion teaching methods are employed to help students discover their own possibilities rather than to attempt to mold them into a predetermined pattern. Moran's theory of teaching method also recognizes that, pursuant to the task of freeing men for an intelligent life in the Spirit, there is a vital need for serious intellectual work in the process of religious education. At bottom, however, Moran seems to place little confidence in any specific teaching method. In a very significant passage he remarks that it is not for man either to control the Spirit of God or to determine man's response. What the religion teacher does, in the final analysis, "is show what a Christian life is by living one."[83]

The Student

Although most contemporary theological theorists appear to be quite aware of scientifically established facts and laws of learning, they tend to rely almost exclusively upon theological considerations in their theorizing about the student in a religious educational setting. In particular, these theorists usually hold that a Christian understanding of man is basic to any valid program of religious education. Randolph Crump Miller, for example, declares that it is not enough for teachers to be acquainted with characteristics and learning patterns of children; they must also consider these characteristics from the standpoint of Christian theology.[84] James Smart, with apparently similar intent, states: "A program that operates with something less than or other than a Christian understanding of persons is likely to produce something less than or other than Christian persons."[85] On the other hand, it should not be inferred that contemporary theorizing purposes to neglect the study of man himself. Indeed, Gabriel Moran pointedly remarks that it is possible to speak badly of God because reflection upon human experience has been superficial.[86]

The student is both a child of God and a sinner

From the perspective of most theorists who have espoused the contemporary theological approach to understanding the religious educational process, the truth about man is that he is both a child of God and at the same time, in some sense, a sinner[87] in need of redemption. Theoretically, this supposedly balanced but rather paradoxical view of the nature of man means that the student in a religious educational setting is neither limited to being the recipient of a salvific message (as in the traditional theological approach) nor does he have sufficient resources within himself to work out his own salvation (as in the social-cultural approach). From this perspective, then, the student is perceived to be an active participant with God (and also with other persons including the teacher) in that revelational relationship which is conceptualized as the core of the religious educational process. Randolph Crump Miller claims that this twofold relationship between God and the student might well be considered the center of the religious educational curriculum, provided that this relationship flows out of theology—"the-truth-about-God-in-relation-to-man."[88] Essentially the same theoretical attitude toward the student may be observed in Lewis Sherrill's statement concerning the nature of Christian education: "Christian education is the attempt, ordinarily by members of the Christian community, to participate in and to guide the changes which take place in persons in their relationships with God, with the church, with other persons, with the physical world, and with oneself."[89] For Sherrill, as for other contemporary theological theorists, the revelation which occurs in this kind of relationship is both individually redemptive and contributory to a sustaining fellowship which is ongoingly revelational.[90]

The student is both a person and a learner

One cardinal principle of much contemporary theological theorizing is that the religious educational process should eventuate in a kind of learning that will be evidenced by the growth and development of the student as a person. (Among the often mentioned distinguishing marks of personhood are: *first,* a consciousness of individual identity; *second,* a capacity for relatedness and fellowship both with God and with other persons; *third,* a capacity for making intelligent, free choices; *fourth,* a capacity to bear responsibility; and *fifth,* a capacity to respond to others—to love.)[91] Such scientifically derived theories of learning as "conditioning," "trial and error," and "learning by insight" are regarded as being largely inadequate to explain or predict those learnings which take place within the religious educational process. Most contemporary theological theorists are of the opinion that practices generated by these learning theories tend to treat the student as a manipulable "object" rather than as a potentially growing, self-conscious, intelligent, free, and responsible "person."[92] While it cannot be said that these theorists share a fully common view on this matter, it does appear that most of them agree that learning which contributes significantly to the religious growth of students is accomplished primarily through interaction between persons (necessarily attended by the as yet undefined, and perhaps undefinable, working of the Holy Spirit) within the relational context of a Christian community which recognizes the freedom of persons to be themselves. Contemporary theological theorists, for the greater part, seem quite willing to concede that learning, thus conceptualized, is fundamentally a mystery.[93]

The student is to become a knowledgeable, responsible Christian

A major intent of contemporary theologically conceived religious education is that the student will be enabled to become a knowledgeable, responsible, adult Christian. To this end, Gabriel Moran remarks that "schools are places for serious intellectual work" where students may begin upon the "road toward understanding" as they are taught to use their intelligence in creative, original, and constructive ways.[94] Beyond the church school, then, the student ought not merely exist as a good and harmless Christian who has been delivered from those ruinous evils that bring unhappiness to individuals and families; rather his task is to participate actively, intelligently, and maturely in God's service through helping other men, giving, in this way, a living witness to the reality of God's love.[95]

In summary, the student as he is ideally perceived by typical contemporary theological theorists, comes from the secular world into the fellowship of the church where he is redemptively exposed to the love of God. Within this community of Christians, the student is provided with access to that knowledge which will both enable him to understand the Christian faith and provide him with a solid foundation for living his adult life as a responsible Christian citizen. Ultimately, he will come to know that the meaning he has found in the church must be carried back into the world through his loyal and courageous Christian living and Christian service.[96]

The Environment

Most contemporary theological theorists, it appears, assume that the Holy Spirit is the determinative environmental factor relative to religious education. These theorists, though, are not unaware of the formative influence of other physical and social factors (home, school, and associates) in the environment. Randolph Crump Miller, for example, states that the scientifically demonstrated organic relationship between man and his environment is transcended by the theologically discovered truth that: ". . . central in the Christian's environment is the living God and that the frame of reference for Christian living is he in whom we live and move and have our being."[97] D. Campbell Wyckoff also considers the existence of God to be the most real aspect of the environment, especially in so far as religious education is concerned. However, he recognizes that a balanced program of religious education must give due recognition to the human aspect and to the natural aspect as well as to the divine aspect of the environment.[98]

The environment, then, is a significant, supernaturally dimensioned element which remains largely in the background of theologically oriented theorizing about religious education. Therefore it does not figure prominently in the deliberative planning of specific religious education practices—for, as Gabriel Moran remarks, it is not for man to control the Spirit of God.[99]

Although contemporary theological theorists do not normally look with favor upon scientifically designed control of the environment as a valid foundation for religious educational practice ("We do not become Christians, as it were, brick on brick through some automatic system of controlled conditioning."),[100] these theorists tend to regard the Christian community, including Christian homes, as being responsible to create environmental conditions whereby the Spirit of God may work most fruitfully in the lives of men. James Smart, for example, appears to take for granted that the environment within the church, and within church related homes, is a critical factor which either helps or hinders the church from accomplishing its appointed educational function.[101] Lewis Sherrill also remarks upon the effects of the immediate environment (the people children know, the things they hear, the events they observe) upon religious learning. The scene of genuine "Christian" education, Sherrill believes, is within the environment provided by the *koinonia* (fellowship) of the Christian community. This *koinonia* by virtue of its own nature includes God as a participant, and it exists as truly within the Christian home as it does within the church.[102] The contemporary theological viewpoint concerning the place of environment in religious education is summarized by Randolph Crump Miller: "Christian education is the process of growing up within the life of the Christian church, and it goes on all the time. The atmosphere in which grace flourishes is the environment of Christian education. With all of our plans and standards and techniques and insights, it is God who does the educating. We are channels of his grace, doing the planting and the watering, and the increase is a gift of God."[103] As with most other contemporary theological theorists, Miller includes the Christian home within the scope of his remarks on environment. He remarks that the atmosphere in the home "reaches the child as naturally as the air he breathes."[104]

Evaluation

Evaluation of student learning outcomes, especially on a day-to-day basis, is not an integral element in the theoretical approach of a majority of contemporary theologically oriented religious educationists. Because it is theorized that a premature attempt to measure progress might well disturb the educational process and actually prevent religious growth, the attitude of contemporary theological theorists relative to assessment of religious educational learning seems to be that such assessment should be only periodic and occasional. The manner in which these theorists shy away from stating definite (behaviorally defined) aims tends to preclude the use of the aim as a meaningful standard for evaluation—at least at the classroom level.[105]

Some contemporary theological theorists have advocated the employment of scientifically founded procedures for accumulating and processing information as a basis for evaluating both religious educational programs and individual progress.[106] However, as Randolph Crump Miller has acknowledged, specifically theological assessment is more in harmony with the principles underlying contemporary theological thinking. Therefore, he offers his opinion that, in the final analysis, when the data from such sources as tests, scorecards, and observations have been collected, these data must be evaluated by comparing them with theological standards. The real question, according to Miller, is whether the things happening in individual lives as a result of the educational program are consistent with the Christian truth.[107] James Smart likewise assigns the ultimate task of religious educational assessment to theology: "The function of theology is to be constantly exercising a critique upon the doctrines and practices that exist within the Church, holding them against the criterion of what God has shown us in his Word . . . and so enabling us to see what ought to be and what ought not to be."[108]

Notes for Chapter IV

1. "Church," "Christian community," "community of Christians," and equivalent expressions are often employed by contemporary theological theorists in reference to the body of Christians united in personal fellowship.

2. As previously mentioned, these hypothetical criteria are derived from a reading of the literature.

3. For an English translation of the often revised *Der Römerbrief*, see Karl Barth, *The Epistle to the Romans*, sixth edition, translated by Edwyn C. Hoskyns (London: Oxford University Press, 1933).

4. Reinhold Niebuhr, *Moral Man and Immoral Society: A Study in Ethics and Politics* (New York: Scribner's, 1932).

5. See D. Campbell Wyckoff, *The Task of Christian Education* Philadelphia: Westminster, 1955), pp. 13-16.

6. Harrison S. Elliott, *Can Religious Education Be Christian?* (New York: Macmillan, 1940), p. 9.

7. *Ibid.*, especially pp. 307-321.

8. H. Shelton Smith, *Faith and Nurture* (New York: Scribner's, 1941).

9. See J. Gordon Chamberlin, *Freedom and Faith* (Philadelphia: Westminster, 1965), especially p. 13.

10. H. Shelton Smith, *Faith and Nurture*, p. vii.

11. Paul H. Vieth, editor, *The Church and Christian Education* (St. Louis: Bethany Press, 1947), p. 7.

12. *Ibid.*

13. James D. Smart, *The Teaching Ministry of the Church* (Philadelphia: Westminster, 1954), p. 65.

14. Sara Little, *The Role of the Bible in Contemporary Christian Education* (Richmond, Virginia: Knox, 1961), p. 12.

15. Randolph Crump Miller, *The Clue to Christian Education* (New York: Scribner's, 1950).

16. *Ibid.*, p. 15.

17. Lewis Joseph Sherrill, *The Gift of Power* (New York: Macmillan, 1955).

18. *Ibid.*, pp. x-xi.

19. *Ibid.*, p. 82. See also, pp. 65-91, 105.

20. James D. Smart, *The Teaching Ministry of the Church*, especially pp. 11-23.

21. James D. Smart, *The Teaching Ministry of the Church* (Philadelphia: Westminster, 1954). This book probably constitutes Smart's most influential contribution to religious educational theory.

22. James D. Smart, *The Creed in Christian Teaching: An Examination of the Basic Principles of Christian Education* (Philadelphia: Westminster, 1962).

23. Gabriel Moran, *Catechesis of Revelation* (New York: Herder and Herder, 1966), p. 13.

24. *Ibid.*, p. 70.

25. Gabriel Moran, *Design for Religion* (New York: Herder and Herder, 1970), especially pp. 11-28.

26. Gabriel Moran, *Catechesis of Revelation* (New York: Herder and Herder, 1966). In this book, Moran extends the principles that he proposed in *Theology of Revelation* (New York: Herder and Herder, 1966) into the realm of religious educational theory.

27. Gabriel Moran, *Vision and Tactics: Toward an Adult Church* (New York: Herder and Herder, 1968).

28. Gabriel Moran, *Design for Religion: Toward an Ecumenical Education* (New York: Herder and Herder, 1970). From Moran's point of view, *Design* represents an attempt to create a new field, namely "ecumenical education."

29. A more recent book by Gabriel Moran is *The Present Revelation : The Search for Religious Foundations* (New York: Herder and Herder, 1972). *The Present Revelation* is a further investigation of the matter of revelation, but it does not touch directly upon matters of interest to this investigation.

30. Randloph Crump Miller, *The Clue to Christian Education*, p. 54.

31. On this matter, see Gabriel Moran, *Theology of Revelation*, pp. 17-21 and *Catechesis of Revelation*, pp. 13-19.

32. Lewis Joseph Sherrill, *The Gift of Power*, pp. 83-84.

33. James D. Smart, *The Teaching Ministry of the Church*, p. 88.

34. Randolph Crump Miller, *The Clue to Christian Education*, p. 37.

35. Randolph Crump Miller, *Education for Christian Living*, second edition (Englewood Cliffs, New Jersey: Prentice-Hall, 1963), p. 55.

36. Lewis Joseph Sherrill, *The Gift of Power*, p. 83.

37. Gabriel Moran, *Catechesis of Revelation*, pp. 72-73.

38. J. Gordon Chamberlin, *Freedom and Faith*, p. 19.

39. On this matter, see Lewis Sherrill, *The Gift of Power*, p. 95; and Randolph Crump Miller, *The Clue to Christian Education*, pp. 3-4, 170.

40. Lewis Joseph Sherrill, *The Gift of Power*, especially pp. 79-86.

41. James D. Smart, *The Teaching Ministry of the Church*, p. 108.

42. D. Campbell Wyckoff, *The Gospel and Christian Education*, p. 51.

43. *Ibid.*, pp. 51-54.

44. J. Gordon Chamberlin, *Freedom and Faith*, pp. 124-126.

45. Lewis Joseph Sherrill, *The Gift of Power*, pp. 83-84.

46. Gabriel Moran, *Vision and Tactics*, p. 75.

47. See Randolph Crump Miller, *The Clue to Christian Education*, pp. 18-36; and *Christian Nurture and the Church* (New York: Scribner's, 1961), pp. 48-64.

48. D. Campbell Wyckoff, *The Task of Christian Education*, pp. 23-24.

49. *Ibid.*, p. 24.

50. See Gabriel Moran, *Catechesis of Revelation*, pp. 100-102; and *Vision and Tactics*, especially p. 118.

51. James D. Smart, *The Teaching Ministry of the Church*, p. 107.

52. Randolph Crump Miller, *The Clue to Christian Education*, p. 5. Miller equates "theology" with the expression "truth-about-God-in-relation-to-man," an expression which he employs widely throughout his writings.

53. *Ibid.*

54. *Ibid.*, p. 6.

55. Randolph Crump Miller, *Education for Christian Living*, p. 44. This particular expression is borrowed from John Dewey.

56. D. Campbell Wyckoff, *The Task of Christian Education*, pp. 52-56.

57. Lewis Joseph Sherrill, *The Gift of Power*, pp. 79-91, 174-175.

58. Howard Grimes, *The Church Redemptive* (New York: Abingdon, 1958), pp. 104-106.

59. See Gabriel Moran, *Design for Religion*, pp. 11-28; *Catechesis of Revelation*, pp. 30-40; and *Vision and Tactics*, pp. 57-68.

60. Randolph Crump Miller, *Education for Christian Living*, p. 173.

61. *Ibid.*, pp. 171-174; and D. Campbell Wyckoff, *The Task of Christian Education*, pp. 50-60.

62. James D. Smart, *The Teaching Ministry of the Church*, pp. 131-153.

63. Lewis Joseph Sherrill, *The Gift of Power*, pp. 92-118, 174-184.

64. Randolph Crump Miller, *Biblical Theology and Christian Education* (New York: Scribner's, 1956).

65. *Ibid.*, especially pp. 1-32. Also see *The Clue to Christian Education*, pp. 3-6; and Sara Little, *The Role of the Bible in Contemporary Christian Education*, pp. 115-118.

66. Gabriel Moran, *Catechesis of Revelation*, p. 78.

67. *Ibid.*, 76-89.

68. Reuel L. Howe, "A Theology for Education," *Religious Education*, LIV (November-December, 1959), especially pp. 494-496.

69. Gabriel Moran, *Vision and Tactics*, p. 72.

70. D. Campbell Wyckoff, *The Task of Christian Education*, p. 121.

71. Randolph Crump Miller, *Education for Christian Living*, p. 369.

72. James D. Smart, *The Teaching Ministry of the Church*, pp. 12, 41, 154-167.

73. See Gabriel Moran, *Vision and Tactics*, pp. 38-68; and *Catechesis of Revelation*, pp. 30-40.

74. D. Campbell Wyckoff, *The Task of Christian Fellowship*, p. 122.

75. *Ibid.*, p. 154.

76. *Ibid.*, p. 111.

77. D. Campbell Wyckoff, *The Gospel and Christian Education*, pp. 147-151.

78. James D. Smart, *The Teaching Ministry of the Church*, pp. 168-169 and 11-23.

79. Randolph Crump Miller, *Christian Nurture and the Church* (New York: Scribner's, 1961), pp. 76-80.

80. *Ibid.*, p. 80.

81. Lewis Joseph Sherrill, *The Gift of Power*, pp. 184-186.

82. Gabriel Moran, *Catechesis of Revelation*, p. 13.

83. *Ibid.*, pp. 67, 70-71; also *Vision and Tactics*, pp. 57-68, 118-121.

84. Randolph Crump Miller, *The Clue to Christian Education*, pp. 17, 55.

85. James D. Smart, *The Teaching Ministry of the Church*, p. 157.

86. Gabriel Moran, *Vision and Tactics*, p. 112.

87. James D. Smart states a typical contemporary theological view on this matter: "Sin, therefore, has to be defined in two dimensions: it is a proud self-centeredness which both alienates a man from God and disrupts his relationships with his fellow men." James D. Smart, *The Teaching Ministry of the Church*, p. 158. Also see Lewis Joseph Sherrill, *The Gift of Power*, pp. 114-115; and Randolph Crump Miller, *The Clue to Christian Education*, pp. 55-70.

88. Randolph Crump Miller, *The Clue to Christian Education*, p. 5.

89. Lewis Joseph Sherrill, *The Gift of Power*, p. 82.

90. *Ibid.*, pp. 65-91, especially p. 78; also Randolph Crump Miller, *Christian Nurture and the Church*, pp. 33-47; and *Education for Christian Living*, p. 7.

91. For example, Lewis Joseph Sherrill, *The Gift of Power*, pp. 1-119; Gabriel Moran, *Vision and Tactics*, pp. 112-114; and D. Campbell Wyckoff, *The Task of Christian Education*, pp. 95-102.

92. See D. Campbell Wyckoff, *The Task of Christian Education*, p. 96; and James D. Smart, *The Teaching Ministry of the Church*, pp. 154-160.

93. On this matter, see James D. Smart, *The Teaching Ministry of the Church*, pp. 156-160; Lewis Joseph Sherrill, *The Gift of Power*, pp. 145-162; Gabriel Moran, *Catechesis of Revelation*, pp. 66-75; and Randolph Crump Miller, *Education for Christian Living*, pp. 41-42.

94. Gabriel Moran, *Catechesis of Revelation*, p. 70.

95. For example, see James D. Smart, *The Teaching Ministry of the Church*, especially pp. 77-80, 103-107.

96. Randolph Crump Miller, *Christian Nurture and the Church*, pp. 61-62.

97. Randolph Crump Miller, *The Clue to Christian Education*, p. 9.

98. D. Campbell Wyckoff, *The Task of Christian Education*, p. 104.

99. Gabriel Moran, *Catechesis of Revelation*, p. 67.

100. D. Campbell Wyckoff, *The Task of Christian Education*, p. 120.

101. James D. Smart, *The Teaching Ministry of the Church*, pp. 168-169.

102. Lewis Joseph Sherrill, *The Gift of Power*, pp. 82-83; also *The Opening Doors of Childhood* (New York: Macmillan, 1939), p. 33.

103. Randolph Crump Miller, *Education for Christian Living*, p. 396.

104. *Ibid.*, pp. 102-103.

105. D. Campbell Wyckoff, *The Task of Christian Education*, p. 38; also *The Gospel and Christian Education*, p. 144.

106. See, for example, D. Campbell Wyckoff, *How to Evaluate Your Education Program* (Philadelphia: Westminster, 1962). This book presents a rather elaborate plan for evaluating the educational ministry of the local church.

107. Randolph Crump Miller, *Education for Christian Living*, pp. 393-394.

108. James D. Smart, *The Teaching Ministry of the Church*, p. 70.

Chapter V

The Social-Science Theoretical Approach to Religious Education

CRITERIA FOR THE SOCIAL-SCIENCE APPROACH

The social-science theoretical approach to religious education is delineated by the following criteria. *First,* normative roles relative to decisions concerning religious educational theory and practice are assigned to an existential fusion on the one hand of both religious and theological conceptualizations in harmony with the prevailing viewpoints of individual churches or denominations, and to empirically validated facts and laws pertaining to the teaching-learning act on the other. Religious as well as theological and biblical content is accepted and inserted as pedagogically appropriate. *Second,* religious instruction[1] is defined as the facilitation of specified, behaviorally defined, religiously targeted behaviors. *Third,* the teacher's function is to deliberatively structure all of the demonstrably relevant pedagogical variables in such a way that the student's religious behavior will be modified along desirable lines. *Fourth,* the student's religious behavior (lifestyle, affective, cognitive) is learned in essentially the same way as any other human behavior.[2]

REPRESENTATIVE LITERATURE OF THE SOCIAL-SCIENCE APPROACH

The social-science approach to theorizing about religious instruction was initially developed in a systematic and thoroughgoing way in the writings of the Roman Catholic religious educationist and teaching-learning specialist, James Michael Lee. That this approach to religious instructional theory is marked by a scientific mentality is evidenced by (1) its commitment to empirical rather than to armchair methodology, (2) its orientation toward objective, quantitative treatment of data, (3) its emphasis upon understanding and predicting behavior (especially religious behavior) on the basis of laws derived from empirically observed and verified phenomena, and (4) its concentration upon identifying and developing (through a process of hypothesis-making and testing) teaching practices by which desired religious behaviors may be reliably facilitated, and (5) its strong theory-practice linkage. Not surprisingly, then, the social-science approach recognizes the findings of the social sciences as a determinative factor in religious instructional decisions.[3]

Several of Lee's earlier books and articles evince a definite, consistent, and recognizable social-science viewpoint toward matters of religious education.[4] A direct, focused application of this social-science approach can be found in a series of three articles which appeared in the fall of 1969 in *Today's Catholic Teacher*.[5] In this series, Lee forcefully advances the position that religious education is more fruitfully conceptualized as a mode of social science than as a mode of theological science.

In 1970, the first presentation of a distinctly social-science approach to religious educational theory and practice to appear in book form was made in several chapters of *Toward a Future for Religious Education*, edited by James Michael Lee and Patrick Rooney. The central thrust of Lee's argument in the key chapter (the third) of this book is that: *"The religion teacher fundamentally is a professional specialist in the modification of student behavior as it affects his religious life."*[6] This thesis has far-ranging implications for the practice of religious education. In the first place, it suggests that the religion teacher, in addition to possessing a knowledge of theology and other religiously related subjects, must be competent to identify with appropriate precision the specified learning outcomes which are desired and to successfully implement the pedagogical processes by which these learnings are most likely to be attained. In the second place, it affords a rationale for viewing the religious instruction act as being value-free because the teaching process by its very nature facilitates behavioral modification about as readily in the direction of one system of religious values as another.

Lee's proposals in *Toward a Future* provoked a heated response from what he has called "the catechetical establishment," the overwhelming majority of whom regarded religious educational theory and practice from the vantage point of a totally theologically grounded perspective.[7] This opposition by the "catechetical establishment" served to reinforce the already obvious conclusion that the approach which Lee had proposed was, indeed, a distinctly different kind of approach to religious educational theory and practice.

Following his earlier foundational proposals in *Today's Catholic Teacher* (1969) and in the third chapter of *Toward a Future for Religious Education* (1970), Lee began to erect what is possibly the first comprehensive theoretical system of religious instruction ever proposed. The framework for this system is most clearly set forth in his trilogy: *The Shape of Religious Instruction* (1971) which provides the basic rationale for the social-science approach to religious instruction; *The Flow of Religious Instruction* (1973) which treats of the structural content of religious instruction; and *The Content of Religious Instruction* (in press) which deals with the substantive content of religious instruction. Lee regards this trilogy as advancing a comprehensive system of religious educational pedagogy which is rooted in the actual dynamics of the teaching-learning act, but which (in contrast to the pedagogy typically advanced by social-cultural theorists) in no way downgrades theological or any other form of religious content. He holds that such a thoroughgoing, comprehensive system is necessary in order (1) that diverse religious instructional practices may be made coherent, and (2) that these practices may be related in both their horizontal and vertical axes.[8]

Of particular significance to religious education as a field—or as a would-be field—is the fact that Lee appears to be the first major religious educational theorist to treat both Protestant and Catholic religious education and educationists alike, in an integrated way. In this chapter, then, the analysis and description of the social-science approach to theorizing about religious educational matters is based entirely upon the works of James Michael Lee, and most especially upon his trilogy, each volume of which is deliberately subtitled *A Social Science Approach*.[9]

ANALYSIS OF THE SOCIAL-SCIENCE APPROACH

The Aim

Genesis of aim

From the perspective of the social-science theoretical approach advanced by James Michael Lee, religious instructional aim is most fruitful when it is determined specifically for each particular teaching situation by the religion teacher[10] in active collaboration with the parents, the student(s), and persons representing the larger church community. When determined in this way religious instructional aim is influenced by a number of variables, such as: (1) family life which has been found to be the most powerful and pervasive variable affecting religious learning; (2) the student himself who is after all the focus of the religious instructional endeavor; (3) the ongoing ministry of the church as commissioned by Jesus Christ; and (4) the teacher's scientifically based knowledge of the possibilities for religious teaching and learning.[11]

The social-science approach, then, does not accept religious instructional aims which are determined solely on the basis of theological conceptualizations. It does, however, give theology a crucial and indispensable role in determining the parameters and overall direction of the religious instructional enterprise. Providing that that theology which aids in the determination of these parameters is a truly Christian theology, it would appear that the practices generated by the social-science approach may be counted upon to support the "benchmark values" of Christianity.

Scope and focus of aim

James Michael Lee agrees with the majority of Christian religious educational thinkers who hold that the ultimate aim of religious instruction is that *every student should live a life characterized by love and service to both God and man in this present world and attain happiness with God in the world to come.* He contends, though, that this generally accepted aim is so broad in scope as to offer little practical assistance in the actual teaching of religion. Lee argues that it is the *primary proximate aim* of religious instruction which exerts a determinative influence upon the selection of religious instructional practices. In several places in his writings Lee describes what he believes are the three major positions relative to the primary proximate aim of religious instruction, namely, the intellectualist position, the moralist position, and the integralist position.[12]

The intellectualist position holds that the primary proximate aim of religious instruction is the intellectual development of the student in matters pertaining to religion. For the intellectualist, religious instruction is essentially targeted toward the knowledge of Christian doctrine and toward an understanding of Christian values (in line with the prevailing viewpoint of a particular church or denomination). Lee maintains that the intellectualist position overvalues knowledge in assuming that if the religion teacher gives knowledge to his students they will thereby become virtuous as a matter of course. Real Christians, he asserts, are not those who know—or even, at a notional level, believe—the right things. Rather they are those who live the kind of life exemplified by Christ.

The moralist position assumes that the primary proximate aim of religious instruction is to make the student in some way more virtuous by bringing him closer to Christ. Moralists typically conclude that religious knowledge is a worthy aim only insofar as this knowledge will be productive of virtue. According to Lee, the moralist position creates an unwarranted chasm between knowledge and action. This position is said to lead to a lifestyle so defective in intellectual quality as to be neither fully Christian nor fully human.

The integralist position,[13] which Lee contends is the one most appropriate for a holistic religious instructional aim, regards the primary proximate aim of religious instruction as "the fusion in one's personal experience of Christianly *understanding, action,* and *love* coequally."[14] He elaborates upon the three constituent elements of this position as follows: "*understanding*" in the full sense of the term is not attained by vicarious means such as study or by being told, rather, it is gained through knowledge plus experience; "*action*" must be understood as a performance which may be either an internal or an external carrying out of a thought, desire, or emotion; "*love*" brings about the synthesis of understanding and action as one person concerns himself with the needs of another. Lee believes that *a commitment to the integralist position will eventuate in a focusing of aim upon the enablement of Christian living as the primary goal of religious instruction.* This focus upon Christian living as the primary goal of religious instruction radically affects religious instructional practice in that the integralist "will typically opt for a primarily environmental strategy, emphasizing product-process, cognitive-affective, verbal-nonverbal, action-oriented practices as they intersect in a prepared, educationally-oriented, total environment."[15]

Behavioral aspect of aim

Christian living, then, is a central theme in social-science oriented theorizing concerning religious instruction. As conceptualized by Lee, Christian living is a broader concept than either Christian belief or Christian love; it subsumes both natural and supernatural virtues and incorporates them into the self-system of the individual and into the *behavioral pattern* by which he lives in the here-and-now. (Lee suggests that the five dimensions of religiosity identified by Charles Glock illustrate what he means by Christian living. Glock's five dimensions are: the ideological dimension—religious belief, the ritualistic dimension—religious practice, the experiential dimension—religious feeling, the intellectual dimension—religious knowledge, and the consequential dimension—religious effects.)[16] It follows that, from the perspective of the social science approach, the aim and emphasis of religious instruction should be upon the total cluster of religious behaviors which constitute Christian living in its entirety. Lee puts forward four cardinal goals of the religious instruction process: *first,* the modification of the student's cognitive behavior so that he has command of religious knowledge and understandings by which he is able to intelligently synthesize his faith; *second,* the modification of the student's affective behavior so that he acquires the capacity to form Christian values, attitudes, etc., as he confronts new religiously related realities in the course of his life; *third,* the modification of the student's product behavior so that he has command of existential, theological, and other relevant subject matter; and *fourth,* the modification of the student's process behavior so that he can ongoingly think, feel, and act in a continuingly relevant Christian way.[17]

From Lee's viewpoint, religious behaviors are learned in much the same way as all other human behaviors are learned (learning being simply defined as a change or modification in behavior). A key tenet of this approach is that religious instruction *"consists in facilitating the modification of the learner's behaviors along desired religious lines."* [18] Facilitation, as Lee uses the term, implies both that the aims of religious instruction must be conceptualized and framed in behavioral terms (i.e. stated as behavioral objectives) and that the assessment of the degree to which the student's behavior is changed be made in terms of performance.

This framing of aims in terms of behavioral (performance) objectives is accomplished through the process of operationalizing. When applied to religious instruction, operationalizing refers to the clear and definite statement of a specified performance from which religious learning can be inferred. Accordingly, the religion teacher who has operationalized his aims for a specific lesson will be able to say both what he expects his students to be able to do at the conclusion of the lesson and how well he expects them to be able to perform this behavior. Quantitative procedures therefore play a crucial role both in the establishment of religious instructional aims and in the assessment of the degree to which these aims are realized as a result of the practices that are employed.[19]

Because of the many problems inherently associated with measuring Christian living in meaningful quantitative terms, Lee has suggested that the most important next step for the field of religious education might well be the development of a taxonomy[20] of religious instructional objectives. Such a taxonomy would classify the full range of religious behaviors both comprehensively and hierarchically. It would be based upon empirically verified facts and laws of learning, and it would incorporate these facts and laws into a purely descriptive set of behaviorally defined statements of religious instructional objectives. According to Lee, this proposed taxonomy would serve a number of vital purposes, such as: supplying a readily available, orderly sequential, and progressively hierarchical classification of demonstrably attainable religious learning outcomes; defining criteria for religious learnings, thereby rendering these learnings operational; establishing a validated base for evaluating religious learning outcomes; and facilitating more effective teaching of religion by reducing the number of vaguely stated objectives.[21]

The social-science approach, to use Lee's phraseology, "is concerned with goals in religious instruction not merely as product ends to be attained, but rather as a set of dynamic learning activities which of themselves lead to the attainment of the desired product and process outcomes."[22] This emphasis upon performance flows from the nature of religious instruction when it is conceptualized as a branch of social science. Lee believes that the relative lack of attention usually given to the operationalizing of religious instructional aims is a natural outgrowth of the view that theology, and theology alone, is normative for religious instruction.

Lee is careful to stress that behavioral modification in religious instruction is not synonymous with psychological behaviorism (after the model of B. F. Skinner or John Broadus Watson, for example). The term "behavioral modification," as employed in the literature of the social-science approach, refers to the attempt by the religion teacher to enable the student to change his specific human behaviors and, indeed, his entire lifestyle, to correspond with the agreed upon aims which are deliberatively formulated to be in harmony with the Christian stance toward life. However, the laws by which these behavioral changes occur are looked upon as falling within the field of learning psychology.[23]

The Content

The proper content of religious instruction is identified by James Michael Lee as being neither more nor less than the *religious* instruction act itself. Because the *religious* instruction act is a religious instruction act (rather than, for example, a theological instruction act) the substantive (subject-matter) content is said to be *religion*. Lee states: "*Religion is . . . the substantive content; instructional practice is the structural content. The substantive content plus the structural content as they are existentially formed and fused in the religious instruction act itself comprise the proper content of religious instruction.*"[24] Delineation of the proper content of religious instruction is especially important from the viewpoint of the social-science approach to religious educational theory because the entire instructional program is rooted in the outcomes which are to be acquired by students. In addition, it is highly important to note that, since substantive content and structural content do not subsist in any real fashion other than in the religious instruction act itself, there exists a fundamental distinction between religious instruction and other forms of instruction. This distinction is a *substantive* (i.e. religious) rather than a *structural* one.

In this work, Lee's views on the religious instructional process (and hence of the *structural content* of religious instruction) will be treated in the succeeding division of this chapter (The Teacher) while his views on *substantive content* will be discussed at this point.

Substantive content

From the perspective of the social-science approach, the substantive content (or, more precisely, *contents*) of religious instruction is religion—a lived experience, not just a conceptualization. In addition to the concept of religion as substantive content, Lee notes that at least three other notions have historically been advanced and concretized into religious instructional programs. In the first place, *theology* has been advanced as the substantive content of religious education. Among other trenchant criticisms which he makes about this view Lee suggests that the empirical evidence indicates that *theology*, in and of itself, does not necessarily give rise to religious lifestyle behavior which is the goal of religious instruction. In the second place, a number of religious educationists (social-cultural, for example) have posited the notion that the substantive content of religious education is *"all of life itself."* A principal shortcoming of this view, according to Lee, is that it carries an immanentist theology to an absurdity. He regards the third notion, namely that religious instructional content is so *"supernatural"* that it cannot be taught, as an unproductive one for religious instruction. If this third view is true, teaching itself is useless. If it is false, it is *prima facie* without any pedagogical merit whatever.[25]

From Lee's social-science standpoint, the experiential quality of the substantive content of religious instruction is underscored by perceiving it as a cluster of interacting contents, each of which may be viewed as a content within its own right.

Individually, each separate content demonstrably yields a different form or mode of learning outcome. The sum-total of all these outcomes added to the outcomes which flow from instructional practice as the structural content is said to form the overall content of religious instruction. These distinctive contents which together form this "cluster" or "bundle" of substantive content include: *product* content, *process* content, *cognitive* content, *affective* content, *verbal* content, *nonverbal* content, *unconscious* content, and *lifestyle* content.[26]

Product content refers to that content which is typically regarded as the outcome (product) of a cognitive operation; it is particularized, static, and usually "tangible." *Process* content, in contrast to product content, is generalized, dynamic, and usually "intangible" in the sense that it is in motion rather than in a fixed state. "A vital feature of process content," to use Lee's expression, "is its developmental nature and thrust."[27] *Process* and *product,* as contents, are not easy to tease apart in any satisfactory manner because they are conceptual rather than existential realities. Like any other instructional act, a religious instruction act is a compound of product and process content fused together, not according to the mode of the product, but "according to *l'existentiel* of the act into which they are subsumed."[28] From another perspective, Lee reminds his readers that content cannot be identified totally with product since both product and process are kinds of content—as well as kinds of messages. Many religion teachers seem to assume that product and process content are identical; whereas, from the social-science viewpoint, process content appears to be a considerably more important learning outcome than product content. This is so, according to Lee, because product content is particularized and transfers readily only to identical situations while process content, being of a general nature, is more readily transferable. Because religion is a process characterized by thin*king,* lo*ving,* and li*ving,* Lee is of the opinion that a major breakthrough in effective religion teaching waits upon the full recognition that process is a crucial content in its own right.

Cognitive content refers to intellectual content of which there are at least three levels, namely: knowledge, understanding, and wisdom. With respect to the cognitive content of religious instruction, knowledge is the learning of the basic elements of

Christianity; understanding is the learning of why these elements are important; and wisdom calls for a relating of this knowledge and understanding to the ultimate principles of existence. Lee notes that it is obviously indispensable for religion to have a cognitive component since man is a rational being. *Affective* content, in contrast to cognitive content, refers to feelings, attitudes, and values. Lee holds it to be apparent that religion teaching ought to include both cognitive and affective contents but that more attention should be given to affective content than to cognitive content because religious behaviors have been empirically demonstrated to be more closely related to affect than to cognition. The research evidence cited by Lee indicates that the affective content in a religion lesson will be enriched by the creation of a warm and accepting atmosphere in which the religion teacher loves and prizes each student for the person that he is.

Verbal content is a symbolic kind of content which tends to mirror objective reality to students instead of providing them with a firsthand encounter with this reality itself. Although it is very helpful for religion teaching, verbal content tends to be ambiguous and abstract; furthermore, it is typically cognitive rather than affective in nature. *Nonverbal* content includes all forms of communication which do not use words, such as the tone of the religion teacher's voice, his body language, and his facial expressions. Nonverbal content is a powerful content which may well be the most authentic and genuine of all forms of religious communication. With respect to verbal-nonverbal content, Lee suggests that the quality of religion teaching in most settings would be enhanced (1) by consciously using verbal content to reflect upon and to analyze concrete, firsthand experience rather than by allowing it to serve as a substitute for experience; and (2) by concentrating upon the deliberate use of nonverbal content in religion lessons—especially because nonverbal communication has been shown to be an effective means of augmenting affective content.

Unconscious content is important for teaching religion because it has a powerful impact upon the color and texture of what an individual learns, especially at the affective level. Lee suggests that the deliberative utilization of unconscious data, such as dreams and fantasies, in the unfolding of the religious instructional act would have a beneficial effect upon the religious instructional endeavor.

Lee asserts that in many ways *lifestyle* content is the most important of the eight contents which comprise the substantive content of religious instruction. It seems obvious that unless there is a definite Christian lifestyle outcome flowing from religious instruction the other contents are quite meaningless. According to data derived from the social sciences, lifestyle content is best taught in a learning situation which is structured in such a way that students learn by living. Among the practical suggestions which Lee repeatedly makes is that the religion class should be thought of as a "laboratory for Christian living." This means that students would learn to live in a Christian manner by engaging in Christian behaviors rather than by just talking about these behaviors. He states at the outset of *The Shape of Religious Instruction,* that: "Christian living is at once the means toward and the goal of religious instruction and indeed of all of religious education."[29]

By thus conceptualizing the substantive content of religious instruction as an interactive cluster of experientially valenced contents, Lee believes that the false dichotomy of "content-centeredness" versus "experience-centeredness" which has plagued the field of religious education for decades can be disposed of once and for all. He states: ". . . a religion lesson based entirely upon process content to the exclusion of product content (or vice versa) is not only existentially impossible but it is totally insufficient for the content of religious instruction."[30]

The religion teacher, then, structures the learning situation most fruitfully when he selects and gives special salience to one content or another on the basis of the kinds of outcomes he desires from a particular lesson. Although the conceptualization of content as a bundle of interactive contents (rather than as a unitary product-content content) is quite new in the field of religious education, Lee maintains that such a delineation will enable the religion teacher to teach more efficaciously. Additionally, he argues that this approach to the substantive content of religious instruction makes it possible for the curriculum designer and the teacher to move more easily toward performance-based religious instructional criteria.[31]

Content-Method

Whereas religious instructional *content* and religion teaching *method* are often dichotomized by religious educationists (especially those who take theological approaches), the social-science approach asserts that these two concepts are one reality fused together in the religious instructional act itself. Lee remarks that earlier conceptualizations of the religious instructional process have tended to look upon religious instruction as a "messenger boy" for, or at best a "translator" for, theology. He contends that these earlier views of religious instruction contribute to the maintenance of a totally artificial breach between content and method. By so doing, these views have also contributed inadvertently, but nonetheless effectively, to a misplaced emphasis—sometimes upon content and sometimes upon method—which has often resulted in ineffective religion teaching.

Lee proposes that this breach between content and method may be healed and that (more importantly) religion teaching may be rendered more fruitful by the adoption of another conceptualization in which the religious instructional process is looked upon as a process of *mediation*. In this mediational activity, both theology and instructional method are subsumed in a sophisticated relationship in which any dichotomy between content and method is existentially impossible. He claims that within this dynamic relationship method and content do not simply add their own properties to the instructional act; rather, they take on the new dimensions of a religious instructional compound.[32] For this reason, Lee remarks that "the age-old method-content duality never really existed except in the heads of religious instruction theorists."[33]

The Teacher

From the viewpoint of the approach to religious instructional theory and practice advanced by James Michael Lee, the teacher in a religious instructional setting is fundamentally a professional specialist who is able to facilitate religious learning. As a professional, the teacher consciously anchors his teaching practice in a theory of teaching which is derived not simply from the facts of learning but also from the facts of teaching. The essential characteristic of the religion teacher, according to this viewpoint, is his functional competence to modify student (learner) behavior along desired religious lines.

The nature of teaching

Like most other contemporary specialists in the teaching-learning dynamic, Lee regards teaching as the overall act which causes a desired change in an individual's behavior. He has defined teaching as: ". . . that orchestrated process whereby one person deliberatively, purposively, and efficaciously structures the learning situation in such a manner that specified desired learning outcomes are thereby acquired by another person."[34] Lee notes that this definition is complex precisely because the teaching act is complex. Indeed, his elaboration of this definition distinguishes among fifteen discrete elements in teaching.[35]

Thus perceived, teaching is, at bottom, a facilitational process. It is an enabling, helping activity by which the teacher, having analyzed both his own pedagogical behavior and the behavior of the student, controls his own behavior with the specific intention of producing desired learning outcomes on the part of the student. The key to optimum teaching of religion, then, is a threefold one: (1) the religion teacher must pay very careful attention to his own pedagogical behavior; (2) he must pay very careful attention to the behavior of the student; and (3) he must exercise skill in controlling his own pedagogical behavior so that it leads to the student's aquisition of desired learning outcomes.[36]

Teaching as prediction. James Michael Lee maintains that because the teacher seeks to produce desired (rather than "happenstance") learning outcomes, he places within the learning situation those variables that he *predicts* will be efficacious in bringing about these outcomes. He states, by way of example, that: "A teacher opts to use pedagogical practice X rather than pedagogical practice Y to produce the desired learning outcome precisely because he predicts practice X will be more effective than practice Y."[37] Although some religious educationists seem to believe that deliberately injecting a predictive element into the religious instructional setting plays down God's part in the religious instructional process, Lee argues that prediction is as crucial to effective religion teaching as it is to any other kind of teaching. He views the utilization of scientifically verified facts as the basis for prediction in religious instruction as a kind of cooperation with God which will result in more fruitful religious instruction. Enhancement of the potency of prediction is, not surprisingly, regarded as one of the most important early benefits to be derived from the social-science approach to religious instruction.[38]

Teaching as a cooperative art-science.   Lee considers teaching to be an *art-science* because it employs both artistic and scientific elements in such a way that the creativity (art) and validity (science) of the pedagogical act is preserved. He observes that teaching which is thus viewed as an art-science has a "built-in generator for pedagogical improvement" since the artist-scientist will have developed the *sensitivities* and *skills* necessary both to observe the consequences of his own instructional behavior and to adjust this behavior in accordance with the *scientific* evaluation he makes about how well these consequences meet his stated performance objectives.[39]

Furthermore, Lee claims that teaching, in addition to being an art-science, is a *cooperative* art-science (an operative art being one which is exercised upon passive matter, a cooperative art being one which is exercised together with an interactive agent). As a cooperative art-science, teaching is a single activity in which the several elements of the teaching situation (teacher, learner, subject matter, and environment) *interact* in such a way that the desired outcome is facilitated. Another reason for regarding teaching as a cooperative art-science is that it is a social activity involving persons. Lee argues that the teacher-centeredness which is obvious in much religious instructional practice stems from the tendency of theologically oriented theorists to consider teaching as an operative rather than as a cooperative activity. The conceptualization of teaching as a cooperative art-science, he believes, will contribute to a desirably student-centered religious instructional process in which feedback from the student becomes an "absolutely indispensable" part of the overall teaching act. To suggest, then, that teaching is a cooperative art-science implies both that teaching is directed toward persons as persons rather than toward persons as objects and that teaching is a joint enterprise between student and teacher.[40]

The teacher as pure function. From the social-science standpoint, a teacher is a teacher purely because of the *function* that he performs and not because of the kind of person that he is. To state that a person is a teacher is to denote that certain kinds of goal-directed activities or services are to be expected of him. For example, one has a right to take for granted that a religion teacher is able to facilitate the modification of student behaviors along desired religious lines. This conceptualization and actualization of the teacher as pure function makes it possible for any kind of capable, willing person to become a religion teacher— providing that "he is able to adequately deploy his personality toward achieving the function which is teaching."[41] From this perspective, the teacher is effective or ineffective according to the degree to which he places his knowledge, skills, and behaviors at the service of the facilitation process. In addition, it should be noted that stress upon the teacher-as-function underscores the helping relationship of the religion teacher and places added emphasis upon the fact that he does not exist for himself but to assist another person to learn to live in a Christian manner. For this reason, Lee states: "The religion teacher ought not to be in the profession for what he can get out of it in terms of personal satisfaction but for what he can give, for what he can facilitate."[42]

The teacher's training

As is true of many religious educationists, Lee considers adequate training for religion teachers to be among the most pressing of the many needs in the field of religious education. Although he assumes that theology and other forms of religiously related knowledge are indispensable to the religion teacher, Lee contends that training programs will dependably lead to more fruitful religion teaching only as they are focused upon improving the actual pedagogical skill of persons intending to teach religion.

In the concluding chapter of *The Flow of Religious Instruction*, Lee concretizes a program model for the improvement of religion teaching.[43] (The concepts incorporated in this two-phase model appear to be implicit throughout Lee's religious educational writings.) *The first phase of Lee's model* suggests that the religion teacher can be brought to a higher level of awareness of his pedagogical behavior through: *first,* being helped to become aware of the theoretical components which operate during a religion lesson; *second,* being aided in identifying as specifically as possible those learning outcomes which he desires his students to attain; *third,* being assisted in ascertaining the degree to which these specified learning outcomes are consequences of his own pedagogical behaviors; and *fourth,* being enabled to analyze the overall instructional act in a critical manner. Lee maintains that this phase of a training program will generate the self-sharpening activity of focusing attention upon the effects of the teacher's pedagogical behaviors as these behaviors interact with the learner, the subject matter, and the environment. At the conclusion of this first phase of his training the teacher should be able (1) to intelligently critique his own pedagogical behaviors and (2) to begin to identify those behaviors which are effective and those which are ineffective in bringing about desired consequential student learning outcomes.

The second phase of Lee's model suggests that the religion teacher can be enabled to achieve more fruitful results from his teaching as he learns to improve his pedagogical behavior. In the *first* stage of this phase, the religion teacher experiments with his own pedagogical behavior in contrived situations which usually become progressively more congruent with a typical instructional setting. As the teacher tries out certain pedagogical behaviors (antecedents) he progressively works toward shaping them so that they become more productive of the desired student learning outcomes (consequences). In the *second* stage, the teacher continues self-experimentation in a practicum or classroom setting under normal, or near normal, conditions. Lee's model suggests that, in the *third* stage, regular practice leads to new and growing analytical insights which in turn initiate the *fourth* stage, namely a heightened awareness of the teacher's own pedagogical behavior. This new awareness serves a dual purpose: to bring a deeper insight into the actual underlying pedagogical dynamic and to serve as a reentry device propelling the teacher back into the first phase of the instructional closed-loop feedback system. Lee's model of instruction as a closed-loop feedback system insures that a teacher training program will be self-generating—at least theoretically.[44]

In summary, Lee holds that training programs for religion teachers must (1) give the teacher an adequate knowledge and understanding of theory, and (2) provide him with the instructional skills (behaviors) by which this theory may be implemented in practice. He believes that training programs rooted in the social sciences rather than in theological science offer the major hope for a bright future for religious education because "it is only from a social-science base that a theory and practice unique to teaching can be developed."[45]

The teacher's instructional practice

As mentioned in the previous section of this chapter (The Content), James Michael Lee takes the position that religion is the *substantive content* of religious instruction while instructional practice is the *structural content,* the *real content* being the "existential compound of both religion and instructional practice."[46] In the present section, Lee's rather extensive treatment of instructional practice (i.e. structural content) will be described under four more or less discrete headings developed from his distinction between learning theory and teaching theory; his proposed taxonomy of the teaching act; his treatment of the structure of teaching; and his analysis of approaches to teaching religion.

Learning theory and teaching theory. Along with many other educational researchers, Lee takes sharp issue with the point of view which regards teaching as merely an application of learning theory. He holds that a teaching theory distinct from, but not divorced from, learning theory is a primary need in the field of religious education. Lee notes that *learning* is a hypothetical construct, a reality which is presumed to exist because it can be inferred from observed changes in an individual's behavior. *Teaching,* on the other hand, is a distinct activity with a particularized set of goal-directed activities. In his view, learning theory which attempts to explain what happens when a student learns is a very different kind of theory than is teaching theory which deals directly with the ways in which one person influences another person to learn. Learning theory which treats of occurrences is a form of *event* theory; whereas teaching theory which is concerned with the means (practices) by which desirable ends may be attained is a form of praxiological theory.[47] Lee remarks that: "Only confusion results when praxiological theory is equated with or reduced to event theory."[48] Nonetheless, teaching and learning are highly related activities which exert a mutual influence on each other in the total instructional experience. For this reason, Lee employs throughout his writings the term "teaching-learning act" to simultaneously indicate the separateness, the relatedness, and the reciprocity of the two functions.

An adequate *theory of learning,* according to Lee, assists the religion teacher principally in two ways: it provides him with necessary data about which variables are affecting learning (performance) at a given moment, and it guides him in selecting (predicting) those variables which will aid him in promoting the desired learning (performance). In his elaboration upon the problems associated with identifying an adequate theory of learning, Lee condemns those theories which have been constructed solely on theological grounds by religious educationists who perceive religious learning to be in some way different from other kinds of learning. The fundamental form of these so-called "Christian learning theories" assumes that it is God who in some mysterious, ineffable way causes the student to learn. Such theologically based theories are held to be so fuzzy and vague as to be of little practical help to the teacher because the theoretical variables that purportedly affect religious learning (grace, divine-human encounter, etc.) are well beyond the teacher's control. A more fruitful approach to learning theory, in Lee's view, is for religious educationists to construct a theory from the facts and laws of human learning as these facts and laws have been discovered by the social sciences. Lee holds that this kind of learning theory, grounded in learning itself, is adequate to provide practical help to the religion teacher by enabling him to select with confidence those variables which will enable him to work effectively with his students in the here-and-now.[49]

An adequate *theory of teaching* which enables the teacher to see that religion teaching is a form of behavioral chaining rather than a mysterious, quasi-mystical event is regarded by Lee as of even greater helpfulness than is an adequate theory of learning. What such a teaching theory does is to suggest which general kinds of pedagogical practice are most likely to be fruitful in certain situations. A teaching theory, then, generates (but does not stipulate) pedagogical practice. The teacher himself fashions specific pedagogical behaviors from the several interactive clusters of his overall teaching theory. Put another way, a teaching theory makes the teaching act intelligible by enabling the teacher to make sense of what happens in the lesson, and it provides a basis for predicting the consequences of the teacher's pedagogical behavior.[50]

A taxonomy of the teaching act. Because of his strongly held conviction that religious instructional practice must be viewed as an important *content* element rather than as merely a *method* of carrying out the task of conveying content, Lee has suggested that a more complete analysis of the teaching act might well put religious educationists in a better position to work toward enhancing the pedagogical effectiveness of religion teaching. To this end he has proposed the development of a taxonomy of the teaching act. Lee believes that such a taxonomy, arranged along a generality-specificity continuum, would: (1) create a deeper understanding of the teaching-learning act; (2) allow for more effective design of instructional practices; (3) enable the development of more effective teaching modes; and (4) help bring consistency to the various levels of the teaching act—so that, for example, substantive and structural content will be mutually reinforcing, instead of working at cross-purposes.[51]

The tentative, preliminary taxonomy of the teaching act proposed by Lee bridges the gap between theory and practice in six sequential categories,[52] namely, approach, style, strategy, method, technique, and step. *Approach* is the most basic orientation toward the teaching act; it is normally inferred from the activities proposed as comprising the instructional act (examples, theological approach, social-science approach). *Style* is the overall pattern or mode of instruction which determines the more general direction and form of learning activities (teacher-centered or learner-centered modes). *Strategy* may be viewed as the overall plan or blueprint for deploying pedagogical methods and techniques (transmission, discovery, and structured learning are examples). *Method* is the set of pedagogical procedures which furnishes the larger tactical units of the teaching-learning act (problem-solving, teacher-pupil planning, affective teaching). *Technique* refers to the structuring of a given learning situation (lecturing, telling, role-playing). *Step* is the (here-and-now) enactment of sequenced pedagogical behavior upon which particularized consequent student response depends (praise, questions, giving direction).

Theoretically, the use of this kind of taxonomy should lead to more effective instructional practice as the steps and techniques used by individual teachers in specific situations become more consciously rooted in wider pedagogical laws. Lee states: "By means of the taxonomy, the religion teacher can radicate his technique in method or strategy, thereby developing a technique which will be effective in his here-and-now lesson."[53]

The structure of teaching.   Lee has identified four major clusters of variables (the teacher, the learner, the subject matter, and the environment) which interact during the teaching act in such a way as to bring about a particular dependent variable (the learning outcome). By deliberatively arranging these four independent variables in as skillful a manner as possible, the religion teacher works toward attaining the outcomes he desires. The goals (aims) of the religion lesson, then, determine the way in which the teacher (or curriculum designer) structures the independent variables. Consequently, Lee asserts that a major function of the religion teacher is to be able to identify those goals which are both desirable and attainable. In addition, the teacher must be skilled in the use of instructional practices which have shown themselves to be fruitful in producing these outcomes.

Lee claims that the four major variables mentioned above may be architected into an overall teaching structure by using the following sequential steps: *first,* specify the instructional objectives in operational terms; *second,* design an instructional system (curriculum, lesson) based upon the best available data about the kinds and sequence of experiences likely to produce the desired goal; *third,* try out the system (curriculum, lesson) under conditions as close to normal as possible; *fourth;* put the system into normal operation after making necessary adjustments; and *fifth,* evaluate the system's effectiveness by measuring the progress toward the instructional goals. Lee emphasizes that this teaching structure incorporates a closed-loop feedback system[54] which generates in-system correctives making the system continually more effective in terms of actualizing the desired goals.[55] This sequential structure of teaching is further developed into a teaching model which utilizes the same essential variables, namely teacher, learner, subject-matter, environment, and goal.[56]

Careful attention to the structure of teaching, according to Lee, will highlight the significance of the antecedent-consequent dimension of the teacher's pedagogical acts. The teacher will then be in a position to use the available means[57] to analyze his pedagogical behaviors with a view to controlling them in order to make his instructional activity more successful.

A prime benefit of paying close attention to the structure of teaching which is envisioned by Lee is that the religion teaching process will be more clearly seen for the complex, cause-effect process that it is. The "veils of mystery" can then be removed from religious instruction as teaching is demonstrated to be a process made up of a series of identifiable, improvable acts. Lee remarks that: "The sooner religious instruction 'despookifies' the teaching act and concentrates on identifying and improving the teacher's pedagogical behavior, the sooner will the Lord, the church, the teacher, and the learner reap the harvest."[58]

Theoretical approaches to teaching religion. In view of his assertion that "a theory of teaching religion is one of the most important determinants of both the kind and the quality of the practice of teaching religion,"[59] it is not surprising that Lee's analysis of major theoretical approaches ("theories") to teaching religion is a central feature in his *The Flow of Religious Instruction.* (It should be recalled that in Lee's taxonomy, an approach is the most basic orientation toward the teaching act.) The major theoretical approaches to religious instruction ("theories") which are analyzed by Lee in *The Flow* are the personality "theory," the authenticity "theory," the witness "theory," the blow "theory," the dialogue "theory" the proclamation "theory," the dedication "theory," and the teaching *theory.*[60] Lee remarks at the outset of his discussion that, of these eight "theories," only the teaching theory specifies the relevant variables in such a way that it has sufficient explanatory and predictive power to merit being called a *theory* in the strict sense of the term.

The *personality* "theory" is said to hold that the sole basic variable in teaching religion is the religion teacher's personality. Lee agrees that a winning personality is an important quality in a religion teacher, but he contends that other, more controllable, variables are necessary for an adequate theory of teaching religion. The *authenticity* "theory" holds that the authentic, here-and-now manifestation of the religion teacher's genuine personality is the basic variable involved in modifying the student's behavior along religious lines. This position, in spite of some empirical support, "imprisons the teacher is the web of his own presently experienced feelings."[61] Therefore it is said to be inadequate as an overarching theory for the teaching of religion. The *witness* "theory" holds that as the religion teacher witnesses to the Christian message in word, deed, and lifestyle the student's behavior will be modified along religious lines. There is the implicit notion in this "theory" that it is the teacher's personal holiness rather than his skill in facilitating religious learning which is the supreme criteria of the good religion teacher. Lee rejects the witness "theory" on the grounds that, among other weaknesses, it is too vague in its delineation of antecedent-consequent relationships in the teaching act. The fourth theoretical approach to teaching religion noted by Lee is the *blow* "theory." This "theory" holds that the incomprehensible action of the Holy Spirit is the basic causal variable involved in the teaching of religion. Lee maintains that the blow "theory" is not adequate as a macrotheory for religious instruction because "its power of prediction is little or nothing, and its explanatory capability is shrouded in opacity and mystery."[62]

The *dialogue* "theory" suggests that modification of the student's behavior along desired religious lines grows out of an interactive teacher-pupil relationship—a deep personal encounter. Lee argues that despite a number of praiseworthy aspects (such as a emphasis upon both teacher-student interaction and process content) the dialogue "theory" is deficient as a macrotheory for explaining and predicting effective religious instruction because it fails to generate a consistent, interconnected series of pedagogical practices targeted toward the specifically religious aims characteristic of religious instruction.

The *proclamation* "theory" of teaching religion is based upon the notion that announcing or heralding the good news of salvation is the primary variable in bringing about religious learning; its emphasis is upon transfer of solid product content. This "theory" incorporates a number of weaknesses in that it pays little attention to learner behavior or to the environment and also that it requires the learner to be largely inactive during the religion lesson. In addition, it generates mostly transmission strategy and lecture techniques. Thus, Lee asserts that the proclamation "theory" fails to meet the criteria of multidimensionality which must characterize an adequate theory of religious instruction. The *dedication* "theory" of religious instruction holds that the teacher's dedication is the most important variable in religion teaching. Lee suggests that this "theory" merits little consideration as a religious instructional theory because it generates few, if any, educational practices. Furthermore, it fails to specify antecedent-consequent relationships at any level in the religious instructional act. Dedication can, however, be helpful variable in the religion teacher's personality structure, Lee notes.

The *teaching theory* of religious instruction, the *theory* advanced by Lee, is based upon the empirically demonstrated causal relationships which exist between the teacher's antecedent pedagogical behaviors and the student's consequent performance behaviors. Possibly the most distinctive characteristic of this theory is that it regards religious instruction as being the purposeful and deliberative modification of the student's behavior along religious lines. The four major variables by which the teaching theory exerts its multidimensional explanatory and predictive powers include all of the pedagogical behaviors utilized by the teacher in the instructional setting; learner variables which embrace such characteristics as intelligence, creativity, affective level, and value orientation; course variables which are comprised of subject matter area, level, and orientation; and environmental variables which include the physical setting, the teacher, and the other students. Lee claims that the teaching theory weaves these four variables into one fabric which both explains their dynamic interaction and predicts teaching effectiveness on the basis of how they are deployed. He states: "The teaching theory of religious instruction . . . raises to the highest level of intelligibility and usefulness the basic multidimensionality of the religious instruction act."[63]

In addition, the *teaching theory* of religious instruction not only allows for but also delineates a closed-loop system of religion teaching. The function of such a closed-loop (feedback) system is to allow for each of the variables involved in the total religious instructional act to interact with all of the other variables "so that the effects of which any single variable has on the next linked variable in the behavioral chain eventually return to the original variable to modify, reinforce, or enhance it."[64] Theoretically, the feedback generated from within an operative closed-loop system leads to a continual self-correction and renewal of the religious instructional process. Evaluation obviously plays a vital role in the processing of feedback within such a closed-loop system.

Finally, the *teaching theory* of religious instruction is directly generative of the *structured learning strategy*[65] of teaching religion because teaching is regarded as the deliberative arrangement of those conditions which are productive of learning.[66]

The Student

The student (learner)[67] is quite possibly the key theoretical element in the social-science perspective on religious instruction espoused by James Michael Lee. From this perspective the student is at the center of the pedagogical act because learning, of which religious learning is an instance, begins and ends with him. Lee holds it to be axiomatic that religion must be taught according to how the student learns rather than, for example, according to the logical structure of theology as many advocates of the theological approaches assert. In this connection, Lee's favorite sentence (since it seems to appear in all of his books) may well be this one: "All learning is according to the mode of the learner."[68] It should be emphasized again that learning, as conceptualized by Lee and other theorists who adopt the social-science viewpoint, is a construct, an inference drawn from observing behavioral changes in an individual. Hence, Lee states: "Effective religion teaching is that which focuses on performance and behavioral change rather than on learning as such. In the final analysis, performance is all the religion teacher has to work with."[69]

The student as a person

It is crucial to Lee's theoretical and practical position on religious instruction that both the natural and supernatural dimensions of man are interwoven together in the student's actual existence as a person in such a way that he is a *whole* self, an integer. This inseparable structural relationship between the natural and supernatural dimensions of man affords a rationale for Lee's insistence that man's religious behavior can be ascertained and modified by using the methods of the social sciences. Religious learning, from this point of view, does not occur within some mystical, amorphous, magical, supernatural dimension of personality; it occurs within the context of an individual's whole personality structure. Lee argues, then, that an optimally effective religious instruction must recognize (and actualize) this wholeness in the make-up of the personality of the student.[70]

The student as learner

Because of the empirical research data which indicate that learning religion is not fundamentally different from learning any other behavior, Lee asserts that the facts of learning which have been discovered and described by the social sciences constitute a reliable fund of theoretical and practical information which is as relevant to the teaching of religion as it is to the teaching of any other subject. For this reason he devotes an extensive chapter in *The Flow of Religious Instruction* to a survey of these findings about human learning and to an analysis of their potential application to the teaching of religion.[71] Lee warns his readers, however, that such findings are not uniformly applicable and that they do not operate in exactly the same way with all learners; rather, they are generalizations which function with differing force according to the particularized, concrete learning situation. Among the most important findings about learning which are touched upon by Lee in his carefully documented survey and analysis are those findings which relate to an individual's early family life, his total experience, his overall environment, his corpus of attitudes, and his personal development.

In the extensive body of research literature surveyed by Lee, the weight of evidence suggests that *early family life* constitutes the single most powerful, pervasive, and enduring variable which affects substantially all aspects of an individual's learning and most especially his learning of attitudes and values. Indeed, moral conduct, emotional life, social behavior, and the entire structure of personality have been found to be determined in major part by those learnings associated with early family living—particularly during the first six years of a child's life. This finding seems to pinpoint the family as the primary agent of religious instruction. Accordingly, Lee claims that its major significance for religious education is that "the religion teacher's role must be regarded as basically a reinforcer and amplifier of the family's work in the religious sector."[72]

A second key finding identified by Lee is that the directness, immediacy, quality, and texture of an individual's *experience* have much to do with the richness, impact, and lasting quality of his learning. Lee concludes that this finding indicates that religion teaching must be saturated with experience which is as direct, as immediate, and as rich as the teacher can possibly make it. The religion teacher must therefore learn to structure learning situations so that the student's learning environment provides stimuli of a rich and varied nature which contribute to the depth and lasting quality of his religious learning.

A third example of the findings discovered by Lee from his investigation of the empirical research on learning is that the *environment* in which an individual develops exerts such a powerful influence that the extent of his learning is actually dependent upon the environment's composition and structure. Because the composition and structure of the learning group environment are controllable aspects of the learner's total environment, Lee argues that much more thought should be given to the direct control of the learning environment than is commonly the case in religious instructional settings. For Lee, the deliberative structuring of the physical, emotional, and social aspects of the learning environment may well be the "most important single pedagogical activity the teacher does."[73]

A fourth finding on which Lee reports is that the total group of *attitudes* held by an individual both shapes and conditions what he will and will not learn. For this reason Lee remarks that teaching for attitudes may well be one of the two or three principal pedagogical tasks of religious instruction. Since the hard research evidence indicates that attitudes tend to be acquired at three pivotal points in life, namely, early childhood, adolescence and young adulthood, Lee argues that great dividends in effective religious teaching would be gained if the overall development of personnel and resources for teaching religion were so ordered as to take advantage of these pivotal points in attitudinal learning.

A final example of these findings on learning is that both moral and religious development are deeply linked with the whole process of human learning and development. This finding, which Lee holds to be so basic as to be almost axiomatic, is of overarching significance for the teaching of religion in that "religious and moral development takes place according to the normal interactive growth patterns of human maturation and learning."[74] This means that religious and moral development does not take place in a magical, mystical, or supernaturally unfathomable manner but according to a discernible cause-and-effect pattern. It should also be noted that this finding underscores the need to "take the learner where he is." Therefore, according to Lee, religion teaching must become a process in which the teacher continually assesses the developmental state of the students so that he may skillfully adapt the various contents of his teaching to their present here-and-now state of existence.

Lee holds that constant reference to these, and other examples of empirically verified findings on human learning, will enable the religion teacher to devise and to deploy pedagogical practices which are, in fact and not in fancy, conducive to bringing about the desired learning outcomes. Stated another way, this reference to the findings on human learning will help the teacher to know "where the learner is at all times" thereby enabling him to become a more effective artist-scientist partner with the student in the unfoldment of the "teaching-learning act."[75]

The Environment

Whereas the environment typically plays an inconsequential role in theologically oriented theorizing about religious education, it is a critical element in the social-science oriented theorizing of James Michael Lee. The rationale for Lee's viewpoint on this matter is grounded in his conviction that revelation, in addition to being a historical phenomenon, is an *"ongoing, present, flesh-and-blood experiencing."* He maintains that experience is not a low level human activity which is inferior to intellectual activity as many theologically oriented theorists assert; rather, it involves the *whole* self in living contact with one's milieu. In the act of experiencing, then, the intellect coordinates with the spirit as well as with the other components of the self. It follows that experience revelationally involves the whole person, including his spiritual, intellectual, and affective dimensions. On this account Lee argues that the religion lesson can be most fruitfully conceptualized as a deliberatively structured environment within which the student's (learner's) experience is recast in a form whereby ongoing revelation is consciously incorporated into this self-system and behavioral pattern of living. Hence, the religion lesson becomes "an environment whose conditions are so shaped by the teacher that a personal living encounter between the learner and Jesus is facilitated."[76]

Facilitation of religious learning by shaping the environment

Lee maintains that the primary mark of a learning environment which has been deliberatively structured so as to produce desired learning is that it is facilitational. "Facilitation," according to his definition, "is the total helping process of enabling the individual to learn for himself all the various 'contents,' the process content as well as the product content, the affective content as well as the cognitive content, the nonverbal content as well as the verbal content."[77] Thus, facilitation involves the deliverative arrangement of all the conditions (i.e. the total environment) by which an individual is enabled to learn according to his developmental level—here-and-now. In religious instruction, the goal of the facilitation process is to provide the kinds of experiences which have been empirically shown to be effective in empowering individuals to acquire behaviors that are truly Christian. The religion teacher's function, as perceived from the social-science standpoint, is to so shape the learning environment by arranging the several facilitational elements (curriculum, social environment, affective climate, the teacher himself, etc.) that the conditions will work together to bring about the intended (and predicted) learning outcome. Lee states that: "It is this structuring of the learning situation to most effectively facilitate the modification of behavior along religious lines which constitutes the very heart of the religious instruction process."[78]

The pedagogical problem when viewed from the facilitational perspective is not to control the actions of the Holy Spirit; it is rather to manipulate the environment (not the learner) in such a way that the Spirit will be enabled to operate most fruitfully. The facilitating teacher, accordingly, bases his pedagogical decisions upon "hard" empirical data about teaching and learning rather than upon theological speculation. For this reason Lee states that: "The facilitation process in religious instruction is a uniquely social-science activity."[79]

In connection with this discussion, it should be noted that James Michael Lee's conceptualization of the religion class as a *"Laboratory for Christian Living"* is a practical way of putting the pedagogical principles of environmental shaping into operation in a particularized religious instructional setting. Lee is convinced that religion can best be learned in a personalized interactive milieu, in other words, in a "laboratory" which stresses such pedagogical elements as primary experience, the here-and-now situation, and person-centeredness. This kind of "laboratory" provides the learner with structured opportunities to live out his beliefs in a manner targeted toward facilitating the "existential fusion" of *believing and living* in a learner's life. A laboratory for Christian living, then, connotes a learning situation in which the learner "hammers out in a deeply existential manner his own personal form of operationalizing the revelation experience in his own life."[80] By way of further explanation, Lee emphasizes throughout his writings that structured environments do not produce desired learnings automatically; they merely facilitate learning.

Environments affecting religious instruction

Within the larger environment which includes all stimuli to which an individual consciously or unconsciously responds, Lee identifies seven environments that seem to be of special relevance to the teaching of religion: (1) the overall cultural climate which influences many aspects of behavior; (2) the local environment which profoundly affects levels of school achievement; (3) the school environment which has the power to stimulate (or stifle) the quality and texture of learning; (4) the classroom or learning environment which exerts a significant impact upon a wide range of learning; (5) the peer group environment which affects the direction of learning; (6) the home environment which exerts a determining influence on value learning; and (7) the immediate physical environment (composed of a host of variables, the most notable of them being the affective climate) which affects the rate and character of learning. Lee suggests that the skillful teacher who attunes himself to the probable effects of these seven environments upon each individual learner can actually capitalize upon these effects in order to sharpen the goal-directedness of student learning.[81]

Although the effective teacher will concern himself with all of those environments which bear upon the teaching and learning of religion, Lee holds that the greater part of his attention should be focused upon the learning environment (often a classroom, but not necessarily so) since this is the environment which is obviously most susceptible to deliberative structuring. His analysis of the learning environment reveals that this environment itself has many properties such as the physical, the social, the affective climate, and the teacher. The *physical environment,* sometimes simplistically viewed as *the* environment, can usually be altered by the religion teacher in such a way as to positively support the desired learning outcomes. The *social environment* is an especially useful variable in religious instructional settings because it can generally be selectively structured in a manner that tends to promote specified religious learnings, for example, social awareness. On the basis of empirical evidence, Lee considers the *affective climate* to be among the more important aspects of the learning environment because it has been demonstrated that it is well within the power of the informed and skillful teacher to control both the form and the thrust of the affective climate so as to predictively facilitate a variety of highly desirable learning outcomes. Finally, Lee believes that the *teacher* himself is "without a doubt" the most significant aspect of the learning environment because the pedagogical behaviors he employs are more highly correlated with successful learning than is the case with any other environmental factor. The significance of the teacher in this regard is underscored by the fact that it is he who gives salience to other characteristics of the environment by the way he structures the environment itself.

Evaluation

Although evaluation of student learning as a significant aspect of religious educational theory has historically played a very small part in the thinking of most religious educationists (especially those of a theological orientation), it has been assigned a vital role in the theorizing of James Michael Lee. According to his social-science oriented theoretical approach, truly purposive evaluation of student learning (1) must be based upon scientific rather than impressionistic evidence; (2) it must be a positive and continuous process; and (3) it must be targeted toward assisting the student to attain desired goals rather than merely measuring final learning outcomes. Furthermore, Lee's perspective on evaluation requires that learning goals be conceptualized in terms of student behavior and framed in terms of student performance (i.e. stated as behavioral objectives). It should also be recalled that Lee holds that religious instructional objectives are most meaningful when they are determined by the teacher in active collaboration with the parents, the student, and representatives of the larger church community.

Evaluation as an integral part of religious instruction

Lee maintains throughout his writings that evaluation of student learning should not be considered the final end of teaching. Rather, it should be regarded as a part and parcel of teaching itself. Thus, in his very first book, Lee states as a pedagogical dictum, that: "Testing does not follow teaching; rather testing is an integral part of teaching."[82] It is on this basis that Lee's previously discussed conceptualization of an optimally effective instructional system incorporates evaluation as an integral factor in its closed-loop, goal-setting, goal-achieving cycle. This whole closed-loop feedback system of antecedent-consequent behaviors as (1) analyzed and (2) controlled by the teacher, according to Lee, clearly shows that evaluation is going on at every moment in the religion lesson.[83]

Measurement in evaluation of religious instruction

Measureable observations of Christian living (the goal of religious instruction) are obviously not always easy to make because of the numerous natural and supernatural variables which affect those behaviors that are commonly identified as Christian. For this reason, Lee believes that a scientifically developed taxonomy of objectives for religious education might well be the key in enabling the teacher (1) to operationalize and state religious instructional goals in a uniform way and (2) to evaluate religious learning according to a reliable and validated standard. By measuring student performance and comparing it with the validated taxonomical standard, the teacher would know the extent of the student's learning, and he would also be able to evaluate the effect of his own pedagogical behaviors. Lee contends that this kind of process by which religious instructional goals are rendered into performance outcomes is necessary because it is only as these outcomes are observed that inferences can be made which allow the religion teacher to know with any sort of validity whether the student has actually learned what was intended. (There are, however, some student *internal* behaviors for which there is typically neither time nor opportunity for the teacher to establish performance criteria. Lee holds that by teaching for process content, the teacher can oftentimes help the student to be able to evaluate these internal behaviors by putting them in performance terms for himself outside the time-space frame of the religion lesson.)

It is James Michael Lee's contention that the kind of sophisticated evaluation described above has never been accorded its proper place in religion teaching for at least three reasons. *First,* the theories of instruction upon which most religious education is based actually do not value any kind of evaluation. *Second,* religious instruction is typically a low-budgeted, low priority undertaking staffed by inadequately trained, nonprofessional personnel who lack the skills and inclination to engage in meaningful (to say nothing of sophisticated) evaluation. *Third,* many religious educationists and other religious leaders hold the implicit (and sometimes explicit) belief that religious instruction deals with the spiritual outcomes that cannot be measured by humanly devised means.[84]

Because of his strongly held conviction (supported by a considerable body of hard research evidence) that adequate evaluation is an integral and indispensable part of religious instruction, Lee proposes that: (1) religious instruction must be radicated in a multidimensional teaching theory that makes integral use of information feedback, rather than in such unidimensional "theories" as the witness "theory" or the personality "theory"; (2) religious instruction must be placed on a professional base with adequate levels of financial, personal, and institutional support; (3) religious instruction must be "despookified" by recognizing that religious behaviors are identifiable and measurable; and (4) religious instruction must flow out of a new level of cooperation between teacher, parent, student, pastor, and all who recognize that evaluation is not necessarily threatening but that it offers the potentiality of new and higher levels of fruitful teaching in the field.[85] Thus, Lee states: ". . . if religious instruction is to move forward, it must make heavy use of scientific, objective evaluation which puts the teacher or administrator is constant touch with his own instructional behavior."[86]

Notes for Chapter V

1. James Michael Lee employs the term "religious instruction" rather than "religious education" or "Christian education" in order to designate a focus upon the teaching-learning dimension of religious education. See *The Shape of Religious Instruction* (Dayton, Ohio: Pflaum, 1970), pp. 6-8.

2. Again, these are hypothetical criteria derived from a reading of the relevant literature.

3. For an extended statement of Lee's rationale, see James Michael Lee, *The Shape of Religious Instruction*, pp. 182-218.

4. See, for example, James Michael Lee, *Principles and Methods of Secondary Education* (New York: McGraw-Hill, 1963); James Michael Lee and Louis J. Putz, editors, *Seminary Education in a Time of Change*

(Notre Dame, Indiana: Fides, 1965); and James Michael Lee, "Professional Criticism of Catholic High Schools," *Catholic World* (October 1961), pp. 7-12.

5. James Michael Lee, "The Third Strategy: A Behaviorial Approach to Religious Education," (three parts), *Today's Catholic Teacher* (September, October, and November, 1969).

6. James Michael Lee, "The Teaching of Religion," in James Michael Lee and Patrick C. Rooney, editors, *Toward a Future for Religious Education* (Dayton, Ohio: Pflaum, 1970), p. 67. Lee stated in an interview that "The Teaching of Religion" was actually written prior to the three articles which appeared in *Today's Catholic Teacher*.

7. See James Michael Lee, Foreword in *Toward a Future for Religious Education*, p. 3.

8. The horizontal axis refers to what might be called the content dimension (product-process, cognitive-affective, verbal-nonverbal, etc.) while the vertical axis refers to what might be called the methodological dimension (approach, style, strategy, method, etc.).

9. Lee's is not the only approach to religious education which can be made from a social-science perspective. See, for example, C. Ellis Nelson's comments in his review of Lee's *The Flow of Religious Instruction* in *The Living Light*, XI (Spring, 1974), pp. 146-148.

10. Lee argues that the religion teacher should be a fully trained professional who works out of a sound theoretical framework. See James Michael Lee, *The Flow of Religious Instruction* (Dayton, Ohio: Pflaum/Standard, 1973), pp. 290-291.

11. See Lee's explanatory note (number 2), *Ibid.*, p. 354.

12. For an extended treatment of these positions, see James Michael Lee, *The Purpose of Catholic Schooling* (Dayton, Ohio: National Catholic Education Association and Pflaum, 1968).

13. The term "integralist" is Lee's.

14. James Michael Lee, *The Flow of Religious Instruction*, p. 11.

15. *Ibid.*, p. 13.

16. Charles Y. Glock, "On the Study of Religious Commitment," *Religious Education*, research supplement, LVII (July-August, 1962), pp. s98-s110. For Lee's application of Glock's five dimensions of religiosity, see James Michael Lee, *The Shape of Religious Instruction*, pp. 11-13.

17. James Michael Lee, *The Shape of Religious Instruction*, p. 56.

18. *Ibid.*

19. James Michael Lee, *The Shape of Religious Instruction*, pp. 204-207.

20. A "taxonomy" is a hierarchically ordered classification of principles and laws. Lee uses the term to mean "an overall classification system of the totality of those behaviors recognized as specifically religious." James Michael Lee, *The Flow of Religious Instruction*, p. 23. An example of a widely used taxonomy in the field of education is Benjamin S. Bloom, *et al.*, *Taxonomy of Educational Objectives: Handbook I: Cognitive Domain* (New York: McKay, 1956).

21. James Michael Lee, *The Shape of Religious Instruction*, pp. 67-69.

22. James Michael Lee, "Towards a Dialogue in Religious Instruction," *The Living Light*, VIII (Spring, 1971), p. 11.

23. See James Michael Lee, *The Shape of Religious Instruction;* p. 63 and *The Flow of Religious Instruction*, pp. 289-290.

24. James Michael Lee, *The Content of Religious Instruction*, in press.

25. *Ibid.*

26. *Ibid.*

27. *Ibid.*

28. *Ibid.*

29. James Michael Lee, *The Shape of Religious Instruction*, p. 10.

30. James Michael Lee, *The Content of Religious Instruction*, in press.

31. *Ibid.*

32. The elements in a compound do not retain their own identity whereas in a mixture they do.

33. James Michael Lee, *The Flow of Religious Instruction*, p. 19.

34. *Ibid.*, p. 206.

35. *Ibid.*, pp. 206-210.

36. *Ibid.*, p. 211.

37. *Ibid.*, p. 212.

38. *Ibid.*, pp. 212-215. See also, James Michael Lee, "Prediction in Religious Instruction," *The Living Light*, IX (Summer, 1972), pp. 43-54.

39. James Michael Lee, *The Flow of Religious Instruction*, pp. 215-218.

40. *Ibid.*, pp. 218-221.

41. *Ibid.*, p. 226.

42. *Ibid.*, p. 229.

43. *Ibid.*, pp. 277-289.

44. *Ibid.*, pp. 279-282.

45. *Ibid.*, p. 294.

46. James Michael Lee, *The Content of Religious Instruction*, in press.

47. "Speculation may be about forms, events, values, or practices. Consequently, there are four kinds of theory: formal theory, event theory, valuational theory, and praxiological theory." Elizabeth Steiner Maccia, "Curriculum Theory and Policy," Bureau of Educational Research and Services, The Ohio State University, 1965, p. 3. Lee's reference here is to the distinction made by Maccia between event theory and praxiological theory.

48. James Michael Lee, *The Flow of Religious Instruction*, p. 57.

49. *Ibid.*, pp. 43-47.

50. *Ibid.*, pp. 47-57.

51. *Ibid.*, p. 32.

52. Reflecting the fact that this taxonomy is only a preliminary one, Lee admits that these categories are less than watertight and that they await further development and testing.

53. James Michael Lee, *The Flow of Religious Instruction*, pp. 230-233.

54. The notion of a closed-loop feedback system reflects Lee's application of cybernetic principles toward an understanding of the structure of teaching.

55. James Michael Lee, *The Flow of Religious Instruction*, pp. 230-233.

56. For a pictorial presentation of this model, see *ibid.*, p. 234.

57. Lee gives a usable summary of a number of available rating, sign, and category systems for accomplishing this analysis, see *ibid.*, pp. 252-268.

58. James Michael Lee, *The Flow of Religious Instruction*, p. 268.

59. *Ibid.*, p. 149.

60. *Ibid.*, pp. 149-205. Lee's analysis of theoretical approaches to teaching religion appears to be without question one of the major contributions of *The Flow of Religious Instruction* to the field of religious education.

61. *Ibid.*, p. 162.

62. *Ibid.*, p. 179.

63. *Ibid.*, p. 198.

64. *Ibid.*, p. 199.

65. For a very practical treatment of the structured learning strategy of teaching religion, see James Michael Lee, "The Third Strategy: A Behavioral Approach to Religious Education," (three parts), *Today's Catholic Teacher* (September, October, and November, 1969).

66. An excellent overview of Lee's perspective on teaching religion is James Michael Lee, "The Teaching of Religion," in *Toward a Future for Religious Education* pp. 55-92.

67. Because of Lee's emphasis upon the teaching-learning process, he commonly employs the term "learner" rather than "student."

68. Lee's views on this matter are treated extensively in James Michael Lee, *Principles and Methods of Secondary Education,* pp. 111-143.

69. James Michael Lee, *The Flow of Religious Instruction,* p. 59.

70. See James Michael Lee, *Principles and Methods of Secondary Education,* pp. 120-128 and *The Shape of Religious Instruction,* pp. 258-293.

71. James Michael Lee, *The Flow of Religious Instruction,* pp. 58-148. This long chapter, with no fewer than four-hundred-twenty-two footnote references, is a mine of information about the empirical research on human learning and its practical application in religious instruction.

72. *Ibid.*, p. 63.

73. James Michael Lee, *Forward Together: A Preparation Program for Religious Education* (Chicago: Thomas More Association, Meditape Program, 1973), twelve ½ hour cassette tapes and instructor's guide, tape number five.

74. James Michael Lee, *The Flow of Religious Instruction,* pp. 135-136.

75. *Ibid.*, especially pp. 147-148.

76. James Michael Lee, *The Shape of Religious Instruction* p. 17.

77. *Ibid.*, p. 49.

78. *Ibid.*, p. 75.

79. *Ibid.*, p. 208.

80. *Ibid.*, p. 81.

81. James Michael Lee, *The Flow of Religious Instruction*, pp. 65-72.

82. James Michael Lee, *Principles and Methods of Secondary Education*, pp. 438-439.

83. James Michael Lee, *The Flow of Religious Instruction*, p. 232.

84. *Ibid.*, p. 275.

85. *Ibid.*, pp. 275-276.

86. *Ibid.*, p. 277.

Chapter VI

The Prospect

THE SITUATION

Both as a field and as a profession, religious education continues to be confronted by a number of longstanding and vexatious problems, some of which are described at the outset of this book. First, there is the problem of *identity:* even the scholarly authorities have not satisfactorily put to rest the nagging question "what is religious (or Christian) education?" Second, there is the problem of *communication:* religious educational leaders have thus far failed to devise either a common language or a common methodology of study based upon universal principles and employing universal categories. And third, there is the problem of *effecting change:* changes in religious educational practice are often made simply by "deciding to do things differently" without reference to theoretical, empirical, or even theological grounds which might justify these changes.

A Starting Point

My initial assumption in this book is that these along with other typical problems are more likely to be solved and the professional status of the field clarified if the entire work of religious education is approached with a conscious attention to theory in simultaneous concert with its application in practice. Proceeding from this assumption, I have attempted to work toward a better understanding of the relationship between theory and practice in the field of religious education (1) by making explicit the viewpoints of major schools of thought concerning a selected range of theoretical components and (2) by making a preliminary assessment of the effects which these viewpoints are likely to have upon the development of religious educational practice.

From an initial examination of the literature, four approaches to theorizing about religious education were identified: *the traditional theological approach* by its view that religious education is accomplished chiefly through the communication of a salvific message to the student; *the social-cultural approach* by its view that religious education is accomplished chiefly through the student's personal participation in social interaction which is purposively aimed toward the creation of an ideal social order; *the contemporary theological approach* by its view that religious education is accomplished chiefly through the student's active participation in the life of the church; and *the social-science approach* by its view that religious education is accomplished chiefly through the deliberative modification of the student's behavior as it affects his religious life. (Although these four approaches to religious educational theorizing appear to be specifically and significantly different from one another, it would be misleading to imply that in and of themselves they are necessarily discrete. The actual boundary lines between them are sometimes not absolutely clear and, more importantly, there are a number of obvious correspondences between individual aspects of the several approaches as indicated from time to time in the course of this book.)

A category system comprising six components which seem to comprehend virtually all of the principal variables involved in any teaching-learning act (aim, content, teacher, student, environment, and evaluation) was employed as an analytical device in an extended examination of relevant works written by theorists representative of the four approaches.

The evidence adduced in the course of this examination seems sufficient to warrant the conclusion that an integral, organic relationship does indeed exist between the theoretical composition of the four approaches and the practices which are usually generated from within them. This finding is demonstrated by the fact that there is a readily apparent difference (1) in the way in which representative theorists perceive that the six theoretical components work together in the overall make-up of the four approaches and (2) in the practices which these theorists tend to associate with each of the six theoretical components.

Thus, there is good reason to believe that a widespread adoption of a system of categories similar to that which I have employed would contribute in a significant way to the fruitful meshing of theory and practice in the field of religious education. Such a meshing of theory and practice should have the effect of enabling religious educationists (1) to bring greater definition to the field by raising religious education to a higher level of professional activity, (2) to communicate more effectively both among themselves and with religion teachers in parish settings, and (3) to establish a more efficacious change process by utilizing readily available scientific methodologies more adequately through the development of a framework for theorizing and for testing hypotheses about pedagogical matters in religious education.

A Perspective on the Field

My major purpose in writing this book, then, has been to invite interested persons to work together toward a better understanding of the relationship between theory and practice in the field of religious education; it has not been to draw far reaching conclusions concerning the relative merits of the four approaches which are described. Nevertheless, because it seems to be uniquely capable of integrating theory and practice on a level which might actually "bridge denominational and theological lines in such a way as to establish valid boundaries for the field," I believe that the social-science approach (or better, some version of it) may well prove to be the brightest hope for the future of religious education as a field and as a profession.

Perhaps my most important reason for holding this belief is that the traditional theological, the contemporary theological, and the social-cultural approaches seem to fall along an orthodox/liberal continuum in which theological conceptualizations typical of each approach are ultimately regarded by representative theorists as fully normative for all decisions pertaining to religious educational theory and practice.[1] Hence, it seems fair to say that almost all of the debate which has taken place across the boundary lines of these approaches has been of a primarily theological nature. This is not surprising in view of the fact that theological issues, in one way or another, have almost always been uppermost in the minds of these theorists. However, this kind of theological debate does not seem to have contributed very much to the actual development of religious education either as a field or as a profession. Indeed, it has often tended to divide the field.

By way of illustration, in the early stages of the investigation which eventually led to the writing of this book I was struck by the considerable amount of time and energy which has been expended by religious educational writers in denouncing (usually on totally theological grounds) all religious educational viewpoints which happen to differ from their own. During the first three decades of the twentieth century, for example, the traditional theological theoretical point of view was a favorite target for social-culturally oriented writings. In response, traditionally oriented theorists strongly defended their own position. Both sides accused the other of not being "truly (or at least 'fully') Christian." Somewhat later, in the decade of the forties, with the development of the contemporary theological perspective on religious educational theory, the battle lines were redrawn. During this period of time, theorists who had adopted a social-cultural stance were forced to defend their typically optimistic brand of theology from attack by writers who had espoused the then developing, less optimistic, contemporary theological perspective on religious educational matters. Thus, the field of religious education has many times been marked more by the sound and fury of verbal broadsides spoken or written in defense of one or another theologically determined theoretical position than by a spirit of wholehearted cooperation in finding ways to make religious education more effective.

On the other hand, to approach religious education directly from the vantage point of the social sciences should afford a better opportunity for religious educationists of differing theological persuasions to establish a definable field. A field so envisioned could provide a communicating environment in which there might be developed and recorded a body of validated information pertinent to the interests of a number of schools of thought. Drawing upon this information, professional religious educationists could devise maximally effective teacher training programs, curricula, and supportive activities which would enable progress toward goals in line with the theological position of any particular institution or organization (whether it is, for example, Evangelical Protestant, Mainline Protestant, or Roman Catholic).

Note for Chapter VI

1. In this connection, a number of individuals who have read major portions of my manuscript have suggested that the approach which I have designated "the social-cultural approach" might better be called "the social-cultural theological approach" to indicate its relationship with "the traditional theological approach" and "the contemporary theological approach." Furthermore, other readers have noted that, while all four approaches seem to be specifically different from one another, there is possibly a generic difference between "the social-science approach" and the other three approaches.

INDEX

Aim, of religious education, 1–5; 30–35; 66–73; 99–105; 130–134
  behavioral aspect of, 132–134
  Christian living as an aspect of, 32; 68; 101; 132
  creative aspect of, 67
  genesis of, 30; 66; 99; 130
  knowledge and understanding as aspects of, 32; 101; 131
  scope and focus of, 34; 68; 100; 130
  social and moral dimensions of, 69; 104
  supernatural element in, 31
  transmissive aspect of, 30
Augustine, Aurelius, 8; 22

Barth, Karl, 95
Bauer, Ferdinand Christian, 60
Behavioral modification, 132–134
Behavioral objectives, 132–134
Benson, Clarence H., 28; 32; 40; 44
Betts, George Herbert, 66; 72–76; 85
Beversluis, Nicholas Henry, 2; 11
Bible, as source of content, 36–38; 76; 109–110
Boehlke, Robert, 7
Bower, William Clayton, 15; 65–86; 96
Bushnell, Horace, 60–62; 95

Carter, G. Emmet, 30; 41
Catechism books, 22–23
Catechumenate, 22
Category system, 7; 9–13; 166–168

Centre International D'études de la Formation Religieuse, 26
Chamberlin, J. Gordon, 10; 1–13
Change, effecting, 6; 166
Character Education Inquiry, 8
Chave, Ernest John, 15; 65–86; 97
Christian living, 32–33; 74; 104–105; 130–132
Church, the, as a theoretical factor in religious education, 64; 95; 100; 130
Coe, George Albert, 10; 15; 64–87; 96
Communication, improving in field of religious education, 1–5; 166
Content, of religious education, 35–41; 73–76; 105–110; 134–151
  arrangement of, 40
  biblical and doctrinal basis of, 36–38; 76; 109–110
  method-content dichotomy, 35; 139
  present living and experience as, 75; 105–108
  structural, 134–135; 139–151
  subject-matter, 37; 75; 108
  substantive, 135–138
  transmission of, 39; 73
Conversion experience, 31–33
Cully, Kendig Brubaker, 12

Darwin, Charles, 60
Deogratias, 22
Descriptive research, 9
Dewey, John, 60–65; 70; 95
Divine-human democracy, 71
Dubin, Robert, 9

171